Trump Judges–
Protecting America's
Establishment Pillars
to
"Make America Great Again"

by

Dr. Jeffrey F. Addicott, B.A., J.D., LL.M., S.J.D.

Lt. Colonel (U.S. Army, Ret.)
&
Professor of Law

Joyce

Jeff Addicott

2020

8111 LBJ Freeway
Suite 1325
Dallas, Texas 75251

phone: (214) 366-1155 / (800) 811-6725
facs: (214) 879-9939
email: sales@ImprimaturPress.com

www.ImprimaturPress.com

Printed in the United States of America

ISBN 978-1-60503-136-1

Dedication

Lt. Colonel R.B. Thieme, Jr. (1918-2009)—

*theologian, soldier, educator, patriot,
pivot of the nation*

Acknowledgments

The author wishes to acknowledge the California Western Law Review and the Dayton Law Review who provided permission to publish selected portions of work from their respective law review journals:

Reshaping American Jurisprudence in the Trump Era – The Rise of "Originalist" Judges, 22 CALIFORNIA WESTERN LAW REVIEW 341 (2019).

The Trump Travel Ban: Rhetoric vs Reality, 44 UNIVERSITY OF DAYTON LAW REVIEW 491 (2019).

Foreword

Jeffrey Addicott is a nationally recognized legal scholar and advocate for originalist, conservative thinking. His latest book, *Trump Judges—Protecting America's Establishment Pillars to Make America Great Again* is a must read. At a time when the country is exposed to endless negativity this book provides a welcomed reminder that America is truly a land of opportunity and tolerance where the rule of law is best protected by originalist judges.

—Sara Carter, FOX News Contributor

Table of Contents

Introduction

"I will appoint pro-life, conservative, second amendment Judges. Justices who will interpret the Constitution the way the founders wanted it interpreted."[1]

– Donald J. Trump

On the cold winter day of January 20, 2017, Donald J. Trump was sworn into office as the 45th President of the United States of America. A moment of joy and great relief for many, but also a time of anger and outrage for others, with liberal progressives and their allies in the main-stream media clearly siding with the anger and outrage portion of the equation – a position they have shown no inclination to turn from. Despite an astonishing record of positive Trump achievements during his first term in office, ranging from a booming U.S. economy to foreign policy successes across the globe, his slogan and promise to "make America great again"[2] (MAGA) is absolutely anathema to them.

Indeed, since a key element of progressive thinking holds that America is an imperialistic ethnocentric nation directly responsible for about every sin known to mankind, they vehemently reject the claim that America is great or ever was great and demand that it be reshaped by an ego-driven know-it-all vision washed primarily in the dye of utopian socialism. MAGA supporters, of course, maintain

---

[1] *Trump: I Will Appoint Pro-life, Conservative, 2nd Amendment Judges,* CNBC (Oct. 19, 2016, 9:08 AM), https://www.cnbc.com/video/2016/10/19/trump-i-will-appoint-pro-life-conservative-2nd-amendment-judges.html.

[2] *See* Pamela Engel, *How Trump Came Up with His Slogan 'Make America Great Again,'* BUS. INSIDER (Jan. 18, 2017, 10:15 AM), http://www.businessinsider.com/trump-make-america-great-again-slogan-history-2017-1.

an opposite view of America and have found a champion in the person of Donald J. Trump. While they recognize that America is an imperfect nation, MAGA supporters insist that since the "establishment pillars" put in place by the Founding Fathers provided fantastic freedom and prosperity, it is high time to recognize, celebrate, and inculcate those pillars back into America's psyche.

Thus, as the nation enters a new decade the country remains sharply divided with the progressive elements of society experiencing serious opposition the likes of which they have not seen since the days of Ronald Reagan in the 1980's. Progressives and their allies know that MAGA leader Donald J. Trump has done their cause tremendous damage and are particularly galled by Trump's appointment of vast numbers of new federal judges that share his vision about protecting the fundamental establishment pillars upon which this country was founded and which produced the greatest national entity the world has ever seen.

One of the factors that is often cited as a key reason why Trump was elected by a majority of the people in a majority of the States was his pledge to the American people to appoint conservative, originalist judges to the bench, particularly when it came to filling any vacancies that might open on the United States Supreme Court.[3] Since the never ending fight for securing an "ideological" majority on the nine-member Supreme Court is always viewed with great concern by both political parties, many wondered at the time whether candidate Trump was simply telling potential voters what they wanted to hear in order to secure their support, or if he would actually keep his word.[4] In turn, others pondered

---

[3] *See* Tessa Berenson, *President Trump Appointed Four Times as Many Federal Appeals Judges as Obama in His First Year*, TIME (Dec. 15, 2017), http://time.com/5066679/donald-trump-federal-judges-record/.

[4] *See* David A. Graham, *Which Republicans Oppose Donald Trump? A Cheat Sheet*, ATLANTIC (Nov. 6, 2016), https://www.theatlantic.com/politics/archive/2016/11/where-republicans-stand-on-donald-trump-a-cheat-sheet/481449/.

exactly what Trump, a former Democrat now Republican from New York, meant by the word "conservative".[5] As we know, as the first term of President Trump Administration's is completed, the firmly stated promises of Trump in this regard can be measured against a factual record of accomplishment.

In a nutshell, President Trump has not only kept his pledge to appoint ideological conservative judges to the federal judiciary, he has largely exceeded the expectations of his supporters and reduced the ranks of the so-called Republican "never Trumpers" to a mere handful.[6] Accordingly, while the objective viewer of the Trump presidency can easily point to a number of impressive Trump successes to include a booming American economy,[7] lowest unemployment numbers in over 50 years, American energy independence, the geographic destruction of ISIS,[8] better trade deals with other nations to include China, lower taxes, stronger military, real border security, and massive deregulation of government agency law, it is the superlative increases in originalist judges seated in the federal judiciary that will most likely extend as one of the most important and

---

[5] Max Boot, *Since When Does Being a Conservative Mean That You Have to Follow Donald Trump*, WASH. POST (Oct. 16, 2018), https://www.washingtonpost.com/blogs/post-partisan/wp/2018/10/16/since-when-does-being-a-conservative-mean-that-you-have-to-follow-donald-trump/?utm_term=.87718a7af535.

[6] *See* Julia Manchester, *Trump Will Be Remembered for Appointing Conservative Judges, Says CBS Reporter*, HILL (Nov. 16, 2018), https://thehill.com/hilltv/rising/417106-trump-will-be-remembered-for-appointing-conservative-judges-says-cbs.

[7] *See* Peter Roff, *Good News Doesn't Always Travel Fast*, U.S. NEWS (Jan. 16, 2018, 5:00 PM), https://www.usnews.com/opinion/thomas-jefferson-street/articles/2018-01-16/the-economy-is-booming-under-trump-but-mainstream-media-wont-tell-you-that.

[8] *Ad-Dawlah al-Islāmiyah fīl-'Irāq al-Shām* is known in the English-speaking world as Islamic State of Iraq and al-Sham (ISIS), although the group prefers the Arabic word *al-Shām* which means Islamic State (IS). *See* JEFFREY F. ADDICOTT, RADICAL ISLAM WHY? CONFRONTING JIHAD AT HOME & ABROAD (2016).

influential of the many positive Trump legacies. The impact will be generational. Progressives know it and are in a state of panic.

– The Coup on Americanism –

America of the twenty-first century is in an ideological battle for the control of its very soul. The uniqueness of what it means to be an American—Americanism—is under vicious attack so that qualities once praised as beneficial to the individual, the family, and the nation are now denigrated and condemned as horrid constructs of the worst order.

Much has been written about various ongoing "coups" to remove Donald Trump from his elected office as president of the United States. In reality, however, the real coup that should concern all true patriots is the ongoing attempt to overthrow Americanism itself. President Trump is merely the most obvious target in a much darker scheme to destroy the establishment pillars that provide the nation with its very lifeblood.

Beyond identifying the fantastic number of new "Trump judges"—both at the federal district court and circuit court levels—that have already passed through the process of confirmation in the Senate, to include two new Supreme Court justices, the purpose of this book is explore not only what it means to be a "Trump judge," but to understand why it is absolutely critical for the continued viability of the nation that our federal courts be populated by lots and lots of Trump judges. In short, with all that can be done to fight progressive policies, this is absolutely one of the best ways to thwart them.

Progressives fully realize the vital importance of securing the federal judiciary. Practically speaking all of their significant advances toward the ultimate goal of creating a subservient society under the thumb of a government that controls the individual from the cradle to the grave have been achieved by a handful of what are termed "living constitutionalist" judges. These judges have no qualms about legislating from the bench. Viewing the Constitution as what Woodrow Wilson called a "living, breathing,"[9] document unelected liberal judges care little for the workings of legislatures or executive actions, either at the State or federal level. Thus, understanding the importance of seating judges that pass their purity test, progressives frantically oppose the appointment of any new conservative, originalist judges. One need look no further for validation of this fact than to the horrendous circus-show during the Bret Kavanaugh Supreme Court Senate confirmation hearings in 2018. Most of all, when it comes to President Trump, progressives are in a state of extreme agitation as they know that he has their number and stands boldly opposed and totally unbowed to them and to their agenda.

Still dreaming of what could have been accomplished if only Hillary Clinton had been elected in 2016, these malcontents rely on living constitutionalist judges in the federal court system to either read into the Constitution novel interpretations that eliminate long standing norms and standards or "find" new enlightened social justice mandates. That is how they work best to fundamentally reshape America into something that was flatly rejected by the Founding Fathers. The ultimate prize is control of the United States Supreme Court. For as the Supreme Court goes, so goes America. Five Justices out of nine is all they need to destroy old law and/or create new law. Supreme Court Justice Antonin Scalia certainly understood the

---

[9]   *See* Mark W. Hendrickson, *The U.S. Constitution: Living, Breathing Document or Dead Letter?* CTR. FOR VISION & VALUES (May 28, 2009), http://www.visionandvalues.org/2009/05/the-us-constitution-living-breathing-document-or-dead-letter/. ("Liberals and progressives believe that the Constitution is a living, breathing document that should evolve with the times. They want Supreme Court justices to be flexible in interpreting the Constitution and adapting 18th-century language to 21st-century applications"); Richard F. Duncan, *Justice Scalia and the Rule of Law: Originalism vs. The Living Constitution* 29 REGENT U.L. REV. 9, 14 (2016).

extreme danger posed by the living constitutionalists and their progressive advocates when he wrote:

> Persuading five Justices [on the Supreme Court of nine] is so much easier than persuading Congress or 50 state legislatures—and what the [living constitutionalist] Justices enshrine in the Constitution lasts forever.[10]

– The Four Establishment Pillars that Make America Great –

One issue that is crystal clear about the Trump presidency is that the onslaught on traditional American values has grown in intensity and nowhere is the associated philosophical fight more important than in seizing control of the federal judiciary. Disoriented to historical reality and even a mustard seed level of common sense, progressives fail to grasp that the underpinnings which established the fledgling nation in 1776 and have continued over two centuries to bless America with a prosperity unknown in the annals of human history are tied directly to an objectively quantifiable set of God-given "intrinsic truths." Fully seen and embraced by the Founding Fathers, these God-given truths are four in number. Destroy them and you destroy all associated prosperity and stability for the individual and the society he resides in. In this light, the Trump MAGA promise is a direct call to action for Americans to not only recognizing the validity of these four pillars but to once again reenergize and celebrate their efficacy.

By adopting four basic establishment pillars[11] as the absolute touchstone upon which to gauge day to day

---

[10] ANTONIN SCALIA & BRYAN A. GARNER, READING LAW: THE INTERPRETATION OF LEGAL TEXTS 410 (2012).

[11] *See generally* R. B. THIEME, THE DIVINE OUTLINE OF HISTORY: DISPENSATION AND THE CHURCH at 28 (briefly mentioning the four divine institutions as volition, the family, marriage, and the national entity); *see also* Buddy Dano, *Divine Institutions,*

behavior, morally flawed beings (a characteristic shared by all mankind) are able to live to their fullest potential resulting in great social, economic, and mental stability for themselves, their family, and their country. Furthermore, the imagined or real imperfections and failures which exist in every human society do not negate the truth or power of the establishment pillars to provide wonderful levels of real good. Societal wrongs in America are merely the ongoing reflection of the wickedness inherent in the nature of man and do not negate the inherent power of the establishment pillars. While no law or set of principles can abolish the bad angels of human nature, the ability of the four establishment pillars to mitigate the damages is without parallel.

As one would expect to be the case, ground zero targets for change by progressives, *i.e.*, elimination, includes all four of the basic pillars that made America great, to wit:

Pillar One: individualism which encompasses freedom, free-will, and the right to privacy;

Pillar Two: the traditional institution of marriage between a man and a woman as the basic corporate bond in society;

Pillar Three: the nuclear family as the ideal environment to raise, instruct, and orient children to truth; and

Pillar Four: the primacy of nationalism/patriotism which includes the vital subcomponents of

(a) limited government;

(b) capitalism/free enterprise;

(c) a strong military;

(d) respect for police and law and order; and

(e) religious freedom of choice.

---

http://www.divineviewpoint.com/Divine_institutions.pdf (detailing the four divine institutions).

19

As more fully explained in Chapter 3, all four pillars are firmly woven into the Judeo/Christian Bible and mixed with religious freedom and tolerance. They are mankind's only path to life, liberty, and the pursuit of happiness. These things made America great and will continue to do so.

While not all of America's establishment pillars are accompanied by a corresponding rule of law which cements their authority into society—nor should they be—the Founding Fathers had the genius to firmly set many of them in the Declaration of Independence and United States Constitution with its Bill of Rights. The former document providing the guiding light manifesto for these truths and the later an iron shield of protection. As a matter of viewpoint, progressives who seek to destroy and supplant the establishment pillars are on the offense and originalists, who support the establishment pillars, are on the defense.

– The Deceit of Progressivism –

Tragically, none of the four establishment pillars are considered as a positive to the progressive. In fact, they hate them. As will be explored in the pages that follow, progressive concepts for the creation of a utopian society are nothing more than sweet sounding siren songs of deceit that can only shipwreck the United States on the shores of misery and doom. Examples of progressive graveyards abound throughout history, but one need not look further than to modern day Venezuela as to what progressive ideology will ultimately bring. Promising a greatness that will far exceed the benefits of the establishment pillars, the misguided masses who fall for it will sooner or later realize that it is all a horrid lie. By then it is too late.

Like Lucifer's distorted promises to Eve in the Garden of Eden,[12] progressives seek to advance their socialist agenda by disingenuous appeals for greater levels of "equality," "brotherhood," or "love" in the social, economic, and

---

[12]   Genesis 3:4-5.

political structure of society. Accordingly, their vision of good for people, society, and government is not only far different, but diametrically in opposition to America's tried and true establishment pillars.

While progressives are extremely active and do great harm with their allies in the mainstream media and Hollywood to denigrate, ridicule, and destroy the aforementioned pillars, almost all of their greatest victories have occurred not in the square of public opinion, but in the federal courts. As previously outlined, by influencing a slim majority of justices sitting on the Supreme Court to simply do away with a given rule of law that protects a particular pillar or to sometimes "find" new laws which advance their own machinations to tear that pillar down they have actually brought the nation dangerously close to an irreversible tipping point. And they know it.

This is why progressives work tirelessly to seat judges that will enable them to implement, enforce, and sustain their agendas. They actively seek out arrogant judges that are self-righteously at ease with dismantling America's establishment pillars by means of viewing the Constitution as a living breathing document that is therefore quickly and easily "changeable" to advance the cause of enlightenment. Such progressive judges unabashedly see themselves as superior intellects and proudly clothe themselves in the fig leaf garments of the elite ruling class. For good reason, when it comes to the Constitution, they abhor originalism and their worst jurisprudential opponent is a fearless originalist judge who holds high the originalist rule of law shield and refuses to bend to the winds of political correctness or pomposity.

Again, this book will define and explore these two diametrically opposed judicial positions and offer a perfect illustration of how this warfare falls out in the legal trenches with the case of *Trump vs. Hawaii*—where a slim majority on the Supreme Court ignored the orchestrated chorus of feigned progressive outrage pushed by the media and upheld the Trump travel-ban, while fending off the emotionally fueled and feckless arguments of the Court's four living constitutionalists. The book will also identify and describe the four establishment pillars.

– Two Elephants in the Room –

Before exploring in greater detail, the matter of Trump judges, it is necessary to note that any discussion concerning President Trump needs to acknowledge that there is, as the saying goes, a very large "elephant in the room." In fact, there are two of them!

The first pachyderm is the main-stream media and the leadership of the Democrat party. Both are populated by the politically correct class[13] and they literally despise the person of Donald J. Trump, all day and every day. While one can understand that the political party not in power would not necessarily be supportive of a chief executive from the opposing political party, the horrendous treatment of President Trump by the Democrat party and their "Resist Movement"[14] has seen a never ending and unparalleled effort to impeach him by any means necessary.[15] The second

---

[13] *See, e.g.*, Charles M. Blow, *Soul Survival in Trump's Hell*, N.Y. TIMES (Sept. 11, 2017), https://www.nytimes.com/2017/09/11/opinion/soul-survival-in-trumps-hell.html (arguing that living in the Trump Administration is the equivalent of existing in a living Hell).

[14] *See* Charlotte Alter, *How the Anti-Trump Resistance is Organizing Its Outrage*, TIME (Oct. 18, 2018), https://time.com/longform/democrat-midterm-strategy/ ("[T]hey're united by a common mission: to oppose Trump's policies, pressure their local Republican representatives and elect Democrats to replace them. . . ."); Tyrone K. Jones, Sr., *Resist Democrats' 'resistance'*, CITIZEN (Feb. 5, 2019), https://thecitizen.com/2019/02/05/resist-democrats-resistance/ (noting the members of the resist movement vehemently oppose President Trump and "reject the fact that he was duly elected as the President of our nation.").

[15] *See* Nicholas Fandos, *Nancy Pelosi Announces Formal Impeachment Inquiry of Trump*, NY TIMES (Sept. 24, 2019), https://www.nytimes.com/2019/09/24/us/politics/democrats-impeachment-trump.html (stating Nancy Pelosi's announcement to initiate the most severe action to be taken against a sitting president, a formal impeachment inquiry against President Trump); Matthew Continetti, *Resistance Inc.*, WASH. REV. (July 27, 2019),

elephant in the room is Trump himself, who quite often engages in hyperbolic tirades sometimes laced with untoward language, even though such words do not necessarily reflect his real intent or view on any given matter. Trump's personality is unabashedly direct and to the point.

It is beyond the ability of this book to chronical the relentless drum beat of anti-Trump vitriol spewed out by the main-stream media[16] and elements the Democrat party.[17] Coupled with the existence of a "deep state" apparatus within the Executive Branch devoted to obstructing the agenda of the Trump Administration,[18] almost every action or pronouncement by President Trump is denigrated by the

https://www.nationalreview.com/2019/07/resistance-inc/ ("Since 2016 an entire media-political infrastructure has been built to push the messages that Trump's election was illegitimate, Trump's actions in and out of office are criminal, and Trump ought to be excised from the government as quickly as possible.").

[16] *See* Jennifer Harper, *Numbers Don't Lie: Media Bias Against Trump is Entrenched, Vicious, Persistent*, WASH. TIMES (June 29, 2017), https://www.washingtontimes.com/news/2017/jun/29/inside-the-beltway-media-bias-against-trump-is-ent/.

[17] *See* Sharon Sernik, *Democrats' vitriol is undoing the party and dividing our nation*, BOSTON GLOBE (Sep. 3, 2019), https://www.bostonglobe.com/opinion/letters/2019/09/02/democrats-vitriol-undoing-party-and-dividing-our-nation/4EWnHMGuWEb2Mahwpnt2VO/story.html ("Democrats now embody incivility, racism, divisiveness, anti-Semitism, intolerance, hatred of Israel, and a level of hostility to anyone not in lock-step with their agenda, and it is tearing America apart."), Desiree Zapata Miller, *Democrats Have Become the Party of Haters*, CHICAGO TRIB. (July 9, 2018), https://www.chicagotribune.com/opinion/commentary/ct-perspec-haters-democratic-party-0710-story.html (" In my lifetime I have never seen hate for those who support a president the likes of which I see toward the supporters of President Donald Trump.").

[18] *See* Julie H. Davis, *'Deep State'? Until Now, It Was a Foreign Concept*, N.Y. TIMES, Mar. 6, 2017 at A19 ("Neither Mr. Trump nor Mr. Bannon has used the term "deep state" publicly. But each has argued that there is an orchestrated effort underway, fueled by leaks and enabled by the news media, to cut down the new president and interfere with his agenda").

main-stream media, causing many to lose confidence in the once perceived ability of these so-called reporters to provide objective or even real news. In other words, President Trump is constantly harangued by a hostile media whose unacceptable level of personal bias[19] negatively impedes those who endeavor to obtain factual, let alone favorable, information about Trump actions and policies.[20] In this light,

---

[19] *See* Jennifer Harper, *Numbers Don't Lie: Media Bias Against Trump is Entrenched, Vicious, Persistent*, WASH. TIMES (June 29, 2017), https://www.washingtontimes.com/news/2017/jun/29/inside-the-beltway-media-bias-against-trump-is-ent/; *see also,* Jennifer Harper, *Unprecedented Hostility: Broadcast Coverage of President Trump Still 90% Negative, Says Study*, WASH. TIMES (March 6, 2018), https://www.washingtontimes.com/news/2018/mar/6/trump-coverage-still-90-negative-says-new-study/ ("Out of a total of 712 evaluative comments made on the air, only 65 were positive, or 9 percent. The rest—647 comments—were negative, amounting to 91 percent."); Stephen Dinan, *Networks' Coverage of Trump Immigration Policy 92 Percent Negative*, WASH. TIMES (July 24, 2018), https://www.washingtontimes.com/news/2018/jul/24/networks-coverage-trump-immigration-policy-92-perc/ (demonstrating staggering negativity across ABC, CBS, and NBC towards Trump's immigration policy); Thomas E. Patterson, *News Coverage of Donald Trump's First 100 Days*, Harvard Kennedy School, Working Paper, RWP17-040, Sept. 2017 ("Trump's coverage during his first 100 days was not merely negative in overall terms. It was unfavorable on every dimension. There was not a single major topic where Trump's coverage was more positive than negative."); Tom Engelhardt, *The Media Have a Trump Addiction*, NATION, (March 27, 2018), https://www.thenation.com/article/the-media-has-a-trump-addiction/ (exhibiting the historic amount of media coverage of President Trump: "no human being in history has ever been covered in this fashion. . . .").

[20] *See* Charles M. Blow, *Soul Survival in Trump's Hell*, N. Y. TIMES (Sept. 11, 2017), https://www.nytimes.com/2017/09/11/opinion/soul-survival-in-trumps-hell.html (arguing that living in the Trump Administration is the equivalent of existing in a living Hell); Jeremy W. Peters, *As Critics Assail Trump, His Supporters Dig In Deeper*, N.Y. TIMES (June 23, 2018), https://www.nytimes.com/2018/06/23/us/politics/republican-voters-trump.html (discussing the harsh responses to President Trump's decisions); *see also* Howard Kurtz, *Behind the Vitriol: Are Trump's Critics Mimicking His Tactics?*, FOX NEWS (April 26, 2018), http://www.foxnews.com/politics/2018/04/26/behind-vitriol-

the media has become nothing less than an arm of his political opponents. Proof of this fact is undeniable.

Midway through his first year, Jennifer Harper of the *Washington Times* added up the media coverage regarding President Trump and published the stone-cold facts in a story entitled: "Numbers Don't Lie: Media Bias Against Trump Is Entrenched, Vicious, Persistent".[21] Nothing has changed. In fact, it has only gotten worse with the partisan media absolutely fixated on finding some way to topple President Trump by keeping alive, for example, the utterly dead corpses of Trump "Russian collusion" or the Ukrainian "phone call" quid pro quo nonsense.[22]

---

are-trumps-critics-mimicking-his-tactics.html (examining the media's coverage of the Trump administration).

[21] *See* Jennifer Harper, *Media Obsession: 55 Percent of Broadcast News Coverage of Trump Centered on Russia Probe*, WASH. TIMES (June 27, 2017), https://www.washingtontimes.com/news/2017/jun/27/media-obsession-55-percent-of-broadcast-news-cover/ (noting the amount of time spent on the Russia matter compared with other important policy topics); *See also* Ed Rogers, *The Media's Mass Hysteria Over 'Collusion' is Out of Control*, WASH. POST (July 11, 2017), https://www.washingtonpost.com/blogs/post-partisan/wp/2017/07/11/the-medias-mass-hysteria-over-collusion-is-out-of-control/?noredirect=on&utm_term=.c3a32fa5ed8a (pointing to different news stations like New York Times and Politico to demonstrate the "breathless coverage."); *The Media's Unhealthy Trump-Russia Obsession . . . By the Numbers*, INVESTOR'S BUS. DAILY (June 29, 2017), https://www.investors.com/politics/editorials/the-medias-unhealthy-trump-russia-obsession-by-the-numbers/ (noting an analysis which found, from May 17 through June 20, the big three networks devoted 353 minutes of their precious airtime to the Russia story —equal to more than half the networks' total Trump coverage over those weeks.").

[22] *See* Aaron Blake, *The Full, Rough Transcript of Trump's Call with Ukraine's President, Annotated*, WASH. POST (Sept. 25, 2019, 10:16 AM), https://www.washingtonpost.com/politics/2019/09/25/rough-transcript-trumps-call-with-ukraines-president-annotated/; Sean Davis, *Like Russian Collusion, Ukraine Hysteria Is Pure Projection by Media and Democrats*, FEDERALIST (Sept. 23, 2019), https://thefederalist.com/2019/09/23/like-russian-collusion-ukraine-hysteria-is-pure-projection-by-media-and-democrats/.

As stated, there are of course other built-in difficulties in assessing Trump policies that are not of the media's making. Specifically, there is President Trump's well-established penchant for engaging in bombastic rhetoric concerning such varied topics as America's border security, criminal justice, NFL teams, "radical Muslims," the Obama Administration's brokered Iran nuclear deal, Hillary's emails, Ukrainian witch hunts, and a whole host of other topics—some significant but others quite petty. Anyone even marginally familiar with the tenor and tone of President Trump understands that he is at times full of defiance and prone to express his views with an acidic passion as if he were at war with everything and everyone, yet enjoying every moment of the battle.[23] It is safe to say that there has never been a more unconventional executive in the oval office quite like Donald Trump, with the possible exception of President Andrew Jackson, who is, quite expectedly, a personal favorite of Trump.

Accordingly, there is no question that President Trump's occasional use of strained monologue has saddled the Trump presidency with many negative connotations causing at times ample grounds for concern, even to his most staunch supporters. Still, it would be naïve to ignore the fact that Trump has an uncanny knack for putting his opponents on the defense where they are then forced to respond on his terms of choice.[24] Clearly, the debate of whether President Trump's lambastic style is political genius or political suicide continues.

While President Trump's personal oratory techniques sometimes appear to run counter to the otherwise laudable

---

[23] AFP, *Trump Tics: Making Hyperbole Great Again*, THE TIMES OF ISR. (Aug. 17, 2016, 4:14 PM), https://www.timesofisrael.com/trump-tics-making-hyperbole-great-again/.

[24] For an interesting discussion of the tension between the "establishment" and President Trump, *see* Alex Altman & Sean Gregory, *Inside Donald Trump's Latest Battle Against the NFL*, TIME (Oct. 6, 2017, 2:31 PM), http://time.com/magazine/us/4960617/october-9th-2017-vol-190-no-14-u-s/ (quoting Terry Sullivan). *Id.*

core meaning of his signature phrase—"make America great again" there is a calming solution for those who otherwise agree with his conservative polices which absolutely embrace the four establishment pillars upon which America was founded. In short, one must listen to President Trump with the eyes and not with the ears In other words, instead of fixating on Trump language the objective observer should concentrate attention on the quantifiable results of the Trump policies. Has President Trump actually delivered in a meaningful way on the promises that he ran on? In this view whether the measure is the economy, military preparedness, border security, tax cuts, energy independence, national security, or support of Israel the answer is clearly in the affirmative, particularly when it comes to his pledge to remake the federal bench with a markedly conservative bent that will help stem the tide of progressive attacks on the four establishment pillars.

At the end of the day, the task for the intelligent observer of Trump policy is to navigate between these two very distracting elephants—media bias and Trump style. While language is extremely important in terms of establishing and projecting policy positions, subsequent actions and results are really the key factors in any assessment regarding favorable outcomes. President Trump certainly advocates a policy of national self-interest and pride in the positive attributes that embody Americanism and appointing Trump judges that protect and advance those attributes are essential to sustaining the establishment pillars.

Chapter One

Originalism vs.
Living Constitutionalist

*"What secret knowledge, one must wonder, is breathed
into lawyers when they become Justices of this Court, that
enables them to discern that a practice which the text of the
Constitution does not clearly proscribe, and which our
people have regarded as constitutional for 200 years, is in
fact unconstitutional? . . . The Court must be living in
another world. Day by day, case by case, it is busy
designing a Constitution for a country I do not
recognize."*[25]

– Justice Antonin G. Scalia

A staunch originalist, the late Justice Antonin Scalia
understood the tremendous power wielded by the Supreme
Court to either destroy or uphold the core establishment
pillars upon which America rests. Scalia also knew full well
that the four establishment pillars were under vicious assault
by progressives on the bench who wished to destroy the
Constitution and all other laws that shielded them. As such,
the often-mouthed fiction that judges are "neutral and
detached" in rendering their decisions is really the stuff of
fairytales and only voiced by progressives when "their"
judge rules in their favor. Ironically, progressives always
claim the originalist rulings are to "shredding the
Constitution" – a document that progressives would love to
tear apart.

While the Chief Justice of the Supreme Court, John
Roberts, often seeks to reassure the public that federal judges

---

[25] Bd. of Cty. Comm'rs v. Umbehr, 518 U.S. 668, 688–89, 711 (1996)
(Scalia, J., dissenting).

are independent from political bias, it is blatantly obvious to even the most casual of observers that Roberts' observation is a goal that is not often reflected in the real world. In his remarks delivered at the University of Minnesota—following the shamelessly absurd Democrat conduct at the Bret Kavanaugh confirmation in 2018—Roberts stated that judges "are to interpret the Constitution and laws of the United States . . . [with] independence from the political branches."[26] However, judges are people and people have ideological/political positions. To ignore or wish away this facet of human nature is naïve at best and disingenuous at worst. Without question, the task of rightfully understanding the importance and impact of personal views in terms of influencing legal rulings cannot be accomplished without entering into, to some degree, the realm of politics and ideology. Then again, in the hyper-partisan environment in which Americans find themselves these days, everything appears politicized.[27] Still, discovering how a particular judge views the Constitution—as a living breathing document or not—will reveal all one needs to know about how that particular judge will fulfill their oath to the Constitution. All judges will mouth the words, "I will uphold the Constitution without influence from politics or ideology," but how they ultimately view the Constitution is actually the *ab initio* key to the manner of how they will uphold it.

To put it another way, to those not inclined to think too deeply on the topic, the general premise of thinking about judges and how they function on the bench is that they must

---

[26] University of Minnesota Law School, *The 2018 Stein Lecture: John G. Roberts, Jr., Chief Justice of the United States*, YOUTUBE (Oct. 22, 2018), https://www.youtube.com/watch?v=9i3RwW0y_kE; *see* Adam Liptak, *Trump Takes Aim at Appeals Court, Calling It a 'Disgrace'*, N.Y. TIMES (Nov. 20. 2018) https://www.nytimes.com/2018/11/20/us/politics/trump-appeals-court-ninth-circuit.html.

[27] *See, e.g.*, Molly Ball, *Nation Divided*, TIME, Nov. 19, 2018, at 26 (describing the bitter chasm that exists between political parties calling it a "fight [that] is about to get even worse.").

set aside their personal feelings and predilections when rendering judicial decisions—particularly when ruling on applicable provisions of the United States Constitution. Federal judges know this is exactly what the general public expects of them and are always keen to parrot the proper language when asked about the matter. Thus, with very rare exceptions, all judges, to include justices on the all-powerful Supreme Court, will adamantly assert that their reasoned legal opinions are rendered solely as a consequence of following "the law."[28] Nevertheless, the informed thinker understands that the law these judges follow is often dictated by their positions set out along an ideological spectrum, which ranges from the conservative originalist[29] interpretation of the Constitution to the living constitutionalist view of the Constitution.

The historical evidence for this phenomenon is obvious and overwhelming. Clearly, if judges really did follow the law and rendered neutral decisions from the bench, then why do so many Supreme Court opinions not only fail to achieve unanimity but easily fall into fixed ideological camps? Indeed, however one wishes to label it, the existence of two distinct judicial weltanschauungs[30] most certainly exists, allowing commentators in many instances to easily prognosticate exactly how, for example, the nine justices on the Supreme Court will split—the conservative vs the liberal

---

[28]   Adam Liptak, *Chief Justice Defends Judicial Independence After Trump Attacks 'Obama Judge'*, N.Y. TIMES (Nov. 21, 2018), https://www.nytimes.com/2018/11/21/us/politics/trump-chief-justice-roberts-rebuke.html.

[29]   *See* Eric Segall, *The Supreme Court is About to Get a Lot Less Honest About Its Fake Originalism*, SLATE (July 16, 2018, 1:45 PM), https://slate.com/news-and-politics/2018/07/the-supreme-court-is-about-to-get-less-honest-about-fake-originalism.html ("[Justice Kennedy] will be sorely missed because, although all the justices decide cases based on their own modern sensibilities, Kennedy was one of the few, left or right, to openly admit it.").

[30]   *See*, OXFORD DICTIONARY, https://en.oxforddictionaries.com/definition/weltanschauung (defining weltanschauungs as "a particular philosophy or view of life; the world view of an individual or group").

wing.[31] The conservative wing will recognize the existence of and support the four establishment pillars and the liberal wing will not.

With all that can be written or spoken about defining the two competing judicial philosophies, when one boils the matter down to the base essentials there emerges a bright line distinction. On the one hand, there are those conservative originalists who assert that "the Constitution is supposed to represent a consensus among we the people in the states [sic], not a national democratic vote or poll and not the policy preferences of unelected judges."[32] While on the other hand, living constitutionalists assert that judges must consider that "rights come not from ancient sources alone"[33]—like the United States Constitution—but also arise "from a better informed understanding of how constitutional imperatives define a [progressive] *liberty* that remains urgent in our own times [emphasis added]."[34] Smug in their

---

[31] STUDENT NEWS DAILY (2005), https://www.studentnewsdaily.com/conservative-vs-liberal-beliefs/.

[32] Duncan, *supra note 9* at 32.

[33] Obergefell v. Hodges, 135 U.S. 2584, 2603 (2015).

[34] *Id.* Kennedy wrote:

> Many who deem same-sex marriage to be wrong reach that conclusion based on decent and honorable religious or philosophical premises, and neither they nor their beliefs are disparaged here. But when that sincere, personal opposition becomes enacted law and public policy, the necessary consequence is to put the imprimatur of the State itself on an exclusion that soon demeans or stigmatizes those whose own liberty is then denied. Under the Constitution, same-sex couples seek in marriage the same legal treatment as opposite-sex couples, and it would disparage their choices and diminish their personhood to deny them this right. The right of same-sex couples to marry that is part of the liberty promised by the Fourteenth Amendment is derived, too, from that Amendment's guarantee of the equal protection of the laws. The Due Process Clause and the Equal Protection Clause are connected in a profound way, though they set forth independent principles. Rights implicit in liberty and rights secured by equal protection may rest on different precepts and are not always coextensive,

superiority to know what is best, progressives view themselves as far smarter and certainly more enlightened than the Founding Fathers. In reality, they are dishonest and not intellectually equipped to run the shoe department at an outlet mall.

– Progressives Embrace Third-Generation Human Rights –

While the living constitutionalist may disdain descriptive terms such as progressive, leftist, or activist, such labels are actually more fitting designations simply for the fact that the living constitutionalist passionately believes that the United States Constitution as originally written by the Founding Fathers is in need of drastic reform—it is "outdated."[35] The answer to why it is outdated is equally apparent—because it shields and protects the four establishment pillars. Thus, since the Constitution is viewed as solidly "frozen in amber" a plain and normal reading means that it cannot address all those "new" and

---

yet in some instances each may be instructive as to the meaning and reach of the other. In any particular case one Clause may be thought to capture the essence of the right in a more accurate and comprehensive way, even as the two Clauses may converge in the identification and definition of the right. *See* M. L. B., 519 U. S., at 120-121; *id.*, at 128-129 (KENNEDY, J., concurring in judgment); Bearden v. Georgia, 461 U.S. 660, 665 (1983).

[35] *See* Adam Liptak, *'We the People' Loses Appeal With People Around the World*, N.Y. TIMES (Feb. 6, 2012), https://www.nytimes.com/2012/02/07/us/we-the-people-loses-appeal-with-people-around-the-world.html. Written charters and constitutions modeled from the U.S. Constitution have rapidly declined. The author cites a study (by David S. Law of Washington University in St. Louis, and Mila Versteeg of the University of Virginia) that concludes:

The turn of the twenty-first century [saw] the beginning of a steep plunge that continues through the most recent years for which we have data, to the point that the constitutions of the world's democracies are, on average, less similar to the U.S. Constitution now than they were at the end of World War II.

"enlightened" things associated with a whole realm of postmodernist agendas such as the progressive's nirvana of a new society marinated in the sauces of so-called third generation human rights.[36]

In contrast to first and second-generation human rights—firmly enshrined in the Bill of Rights—which prohibit the central government from engaging in certain clearly defined acts against its citizens depriving them of life, liberty, or private property interests, third generation human rights are the exact polar opposite. Instead of "thou shalt not" prohibitions to the government which make up first and second-generation human rights, third-generation rights are "thou shalt" commands for an omnipotent government to provide certain social and welfare benefits to all. Third-generation human rights include such socialist "rights" as free social security, free education, free health care, free resource development, free food, free humanitarian assistance, and even free income. In short, it is socialism/communism.

Ironically, those nations that foolishly embrace third-generation rights soon discover that they sacrifice on the altar of the "greater good" their first and second-generation human rights. In order to function, the socialist government must confiscate private property as well as the means of production of wealth. The greater good mantra which underpins third-generation human rights must sooner or later crush individual liberties as it tears down the four establishment pillars. The State becomes more important than the individual citizen because the State does not exist to serve the individual, the individual exists to serve the State.

Thus, in order to rectify the matter of rigidity imbedded in the U.S. Constitution, which protects the four pillars, the liberal judge is obliged to reinvent the Constitution into a

---

[36] *See* JEFFREY F. ADDICOTT, TERRORISM LAW: MATERIALS, CASES, COMMENTS 367-368 (7th ed. 2014).

"living, breathing, document,"[37] allowing them to make out of whole cloth any and every interpretation that is in accordance with whatever set of "desirable" progressive norms that they wish to foist on the country. Clearly, this fluid methodology of pseudo-interpretation is fueled by and embraces a broader progressive movement which cannot coexist with the freedom provisions of the original document. Not only does the living constitutionalist feel that the Constitution should not be viewed as a collection of fixed mandates and laws, for them it serves as an open invitation to apply contemporary meanings, standards, and norms. Washed in platitudes about equality and social justice, the progressive federal judge imposes his will on the people.

Naturally, the progressive living constitutionalist judge will seldom admit to their schemes or openly attack the Constitution, he will simply cover his actions by presenting justifications washed in enlightenment nonsense. For instance, in the 2015 landmark case of *Obergefell v. Hodges*, a 5-4 ruling by the Supreme Court, Justice Kennedy provided the tie breaking swing vote to require States to perform and recognize the "marriages" of same-sex couples. Despite the fact that every State—to include deep blue California—that had previously considered the matter flatly rejected it at the ballot box, living constitutionalist Supreme Court justices somehow discovered this new interpretation of marriage hidden right there in plain sight under the "Due Process Clause" and the "Equal Protection Clause" of the Fourteenth Amendment. When Kennedy joined the ranks of the four committed living constitutionalists on the Court, he eliminated the right of the American people to determine such foundational matters in the culture and society where they live. Kennedy self-righteously wrote that same-sex marriage was a sacred "constitutional imperative"—even if it wasn't actually in the Constitution—and that the

---

[37] *See* Joe Carter, *Justice Scalia Explains Why the 'Living Constitution' is a Threat to America*, ACTON INST. (May 14, 2018), http://blog.acton.org/archives/101616-justice-scalia-explains-why-the-living-constitution-is-a-threat-to-america.html.

traditional views about marriage which had existed from time immemorial had to be redefined to include homosexual partnerships. In fact, it was an urgent imperative "in our own era."

> The right to marry [between a man and a woman] is fundamental as a matter of history and tradition, but rights come not from ancient sources alone [e.g., the Constitution or the Bible]. They rise, too, from a *better-informed understanding of how constitutional imperatives define a liberty that remains urgent in our own era* [emphasis added].[38]

Kennedy then went on to imperiously explain that only progressives were qualified to substitute their enlightened view over the Constitution and the will of the people to determine, as he put it "what freedom is," and regardless of what the Constitution might otherwise say, what freedom "must become." He had the audacity to admit:

> This interrelation of the two principles [the Due Process and Equal Protection clauses] furthers our [progressives] understanding of what freedom is and must become.[39]

In the words of living constitutionalist Supreme Court Justice Ruth Ginsburg, who is widely celebrated by progressives as the darling head of the liberal wing of the Court,[40] a plain and normal originalist reading of the U.S. Constitution does not provide the necessary flexibility, i.e.,

---

[38] Obergefell v. Hodges, 135 U.S. 2584, 2603 (2015).

[39] *Id.*

[40] *See* Stephanie F. Ward, *Justice Ruth Bader Ginsburg Has Become an Unlikely Pop Culture Icon*, ABA J. (Oct. 2018), http://www.abajournal.com/magazine/article/ruth_bader_ginsburg_pop _culture_icon; *see also* Samantha Schmidt, *Ruth Bader Ginsburg Says She Has 'At Least 5 More Years' on the Supreme Court. Her Fans Rejoice.*, WASH. POST (July 30, 2018), https://www.washingtonpost.com/news/morning-mix/wp/2018/07/30/ ruth-bader-ginsburg-says-she-has-at-least-5-more-years-on-the-supreme-court-her-fans-rejoice/?utm_term=.b7ed4dab84db.

ability to change, when it comes to addressing these new social imperatives "urgent in our own era." Like all progressives, Ginsburg is equally bewitched and enamored by the supremacy of third-generation human rights. For instance, in a 2012 interview given to an Egyptian TV station Ginsburg freely admitted that if Egypt were drafting a new constitution (in the wake of the Moslem Brotherhood takeover of the government) that she would "not look to the U.S. Constitution" for guidance:

> You [those tasked with drafting the anticipated new Egyptian constitution] should certainly be aided by all the constitution writing that has gone on since the end of World War II. I would not look to the U.S. Constitution if I were drafting a constitution in 2012. I might look to the constitution of South Africa. That was a deliberate attempt to have a fundamental instrument of government that embraced basic human rights, had an independent judiciary. . . It really is, I think, a great piece of work that was done. Much more recent than the U.S. Constitution— Canada has a Charter of Rights and Freedoms. It dates from 1982. You would almost certainly look at the European Convention on Human Rights.[41]

Setting aside the issue of praising a given third-generation human right, the South African constitution heralded by Justice Ginsburg is extremely complex, and with well over 100 pages is far too fluid to actually function in the real world. Attempting to address every possible legal scenario one might imagine, the document is basically impossible to translate into reality. In contrast, the beauty of the U.S. Constitution is that it is short and simple. Recognizing that rules are made for the general principle and not for every conceivable exigency of life, the Founding

---

[41] *See U.S. Supreme Court Justice Ruth Bader Ginsburg to Egyptians: Look to the Constitutions of South Africa or Canada, not to the U.S. Constitution, as a Model*, MIDDLE E. MEDIA RES. INST. (Feb. 7, 2012), https://www.memri.org/reports/us-supreme-court-justice-ruth-bader-ginsburg-egyptians-look-constitutions-south-africa-or.

Fathers intended that the real power in the U.S. Constitution must rest in the people, not in unelected Supreme Court Justices or an all-powerful central government.

Those progressives who have the temerity to interpret the U.S. Constitution as a document that can mean anything, means, of course, that it means nothing. By definition, such a bizarre intellectual position about the meaning of the Constitution is the devil's own playground. There is no predictability of outcome. While some imagined readings might produce some temporary societal good in the short term, it will most certainly also produce great harm—sooner rather than later.

– Originalist Embrace
the Establishment Pillars –

In contrast to the living constitutionalist, the originalist is primarily concerned with what the writers meant when they drafted the Constitution and the attendant amendments, not what subsequent readers might want those words to mean. Greatly valuing the genius of the Founding Fathers, the originalist seeks to comprehend with as much precision as possible the original intent of the author(s) and does not agree with the idea that the U.S. Constitution and Bill of Rights are now outmoded or will ever be outmoded in terms of addressing the key issues of providing prosperity and liberty to its people. They wisely perceive the intrinsic truth of the four establishment pillars upon which America was constructed. Thus, an originalist then is best defined as one who believes that the actual text of the United States Constitution should be interpreted based on the intent of the authors and the context surrounding the creation of the document.[42]   Simply put: "What did the author of the document intend?"

---

[42]   Yvonne Tew, *Originalism at Home and Abroad*, 52 COLUM. J. TRANSNAT'L L. 780, 789 (2014); *see also* Steven Calabresi, *Originalism in Constitutional Interpretation*, https://constitutioncenter.org/

Understanding the destructive flaws inherent in human nature, a central commonality of all major religions, the originalist agrees that the U.S. Constitution constructively addresses the attendant challenges of sustaining a limited governmental system of authority that provides basic protections from an overreaching and too powerful central government. He absolutely rejects, as a "fraud and a delusion,"[43] the living constitutionalist who is viewed as nothing more than a ravenous wolf in sheep's clothing—mouthing support for the Constitution but secretly despising its rigidity.

Interestingly, Justice Scalia often exposed the intellectual gymnastics engaged in by living constitutionalists when they sought to cover their machinations. While progressives complain that the Constitution as written is inflexible and must be made more pliable in the modern age, it is they who actually make the Constitution absolutely inflexible. Remember, it is the living constitutionalist who seeks to eliminate the four establishment pillars which means that there is then no debate whatsoever about the matter at the ballot box or anywhere else. Scalia wrote:

> [T]he notion that the advocates of the Living Constitution want to bring us flexibility and openness to change is a fraud and a delusion. All one needs for flexibility and change is a ballot box and a legislature. The advocates of the Living Constitution want to bring us what constitutions are designed to impart: rigidity and difficulty of change. The originalists' Constitution produces a flexible and adaptable political system. Do the people want the death penalty? The Constitution neither requires nor forbids it, so they can impose or abolish it, as they wish. And they can change their mind—abolishing

interactive-constitution/white-pages/on-originalism-in-constitutional-interpretation.

[43]   SCALIA & GARNER, *supra* note 10, at 410.

it and then reinstituting it when the incidence of murder increases. When, however, living constitutionalists read a prohibition of the death penalty into the Constitution . . . all flexibility is at an end. It would thereafter be of no use debating the merits of the death penalty, just as it is of no use debating the merits of prohibiting abortion. The subject has simply been eliminated from the arena of democratic choice. And that is not, we emphasize, an accidental consequence of the Living Constitution: It is the whole purpose that this fictitious construct is designed to serve. Persuading five Justices is so much easier than persuading Congress or 50 state legislatures—and what the Justices enshrine in the Constitution lasts forever. In practice, the Living Constitution would better be called the Dead Democracy.[44]

Finally, originalists need not fret about charges that they are bending the words of the Constitution to match their own ideology, a charge correctly leveled at the progressives. The fact of the matter is that the Constitution contains within its DNA the four establishment pillars. It reflects conservative ideology from stem to stern.

– The Literalist –

Although conservatives embrace the appointment of men and women to the federal bench who embrace originalism, this is not to be confused with "literalism" or, alternatively, that they view themselves as intellectually locked into the physical historical conditions of a bygone age. Indeed, since the writer of the document might employ a variety of literary techniques to enshrine his thoughts on paper, the originalist is apt to shun the literalist as much as he shuns the living constitutionalist.

---

[44]   SCALIA & GARNER, *supra* note 10, at 410.

Because the overarching desire of the originalist is to capture the exact thought of the drafter, they consider the legal matter in question under the rubric of isagogical,[45] categorical, and exegetical[46] (ICE)[47] thinking, whereas the literalist might simply attach a literal reading. Without fully understanding and applying the ICE factors to arrive at a true interpretation, the literalist, who only narrowly views the words as written, can arrive at bizarre conclusions. For example, many are familiar with the words of Jesus of Nazareth spoken at the Sermon on the Mount (The Beatitudes) calling on a man to cut off his hand if it "made him stumble."[48] Obviously, this verse should not be taken literally. In the gospel of Matthew, Jesus said:

> If your right hand makes you stumble, cut it off and throw it from you; for it is better for you to lose one of the parts of your body, than for your whole body to go into hell.[49]

Without too much intellectual effort, the ICE scholar understands that Jesus, who repeatedly claimed to be the

---

[45] *See* MERRIAM-WEBSTER, https://www.merriam-webster.com/dictionary/isagogics (defining "isagogics" as the "introductory study of a branch of theology that is preliminary to actual exegesis and deals with the literary and external history of the Bible").

[46] *See*, OXFORD DICTIONARY, https://en.oxforddictionaries.com/definition/exegesis (defining "exegetical" as "critical explanation or interpretation of a text, especially of scripture").

[47] The acronym ICE was promoted by the late Biblical scholar and Pastor/Teacher Lt. Colonel R. B. Thieme, Jr. *See, e.g.*, JOHN LAYTON WALL, BOB THIEME'S TEACHINGS ON CHRISTIAN LIVING (1978) (published Th.D. dissertation, Church Multiplication, Inc.), http://withchrist.org/thieme_by_joe_wall.pdf; *The Importance of Doctrine*, WEST BANK BIBLE CHURCH, http://www.westbankbiblechurch.com/LGMerrittBooks/091113 Importance%20of%20Doctrine.pdf; (last visited Mar. 30, 2019).

[48] Matt. 5:30 (New American Standard Version).

[49] *Id.*

promised Messiah[50]—the lamb of God who would take away the sin of the world by bearing in His own body all human sin (past, present, and future)[51]—was providing an illustrative warning that nothing in this short life should stand in the way of a person accepting God's unconditional and free offer of salvation by grace,[52] as the alternative is to spend eternity in separation from their Creator.

Admittedly, the Supreme Court itself has sometimes fallen prey to literalism. For example, in 1928 the Supreme Court in *Olmstead v. United States*[53] ruled on the constitutionality of law enforcement "wiretapping" the telephones of individuals in their homes without a search warrant.[54] Because there were no phones at the time of the adoption of the Fourth Amendment in 1791, the Court essentially ruled that there was no protected right to privacy because wiretapping did not constitute an actual physical intrusion of the person or property. As a consequence of this ruling law enforcement dramatically increased the use of wiretaps, prompting Congress to intervene with protecting legislation[55] which subsequently led to the 1967 landmark privacy decision of *Katz v. United States*.[56] *Katz* held that Fourth Amendment protections extended to government

---

[50] The Greek word *christos* is the exact equivalent of the Hebrew word *messiah*. The English translation is Christ.

[51] *See* Jn. 1:29: "The next day he [John the Baptist] saw Jesus coming to him and said, 'Behold, the Lamb of God who takes away the sin of the world!'").

[52] *See* KATHERINE STARK TAPPING & CATHERINE BRADEN YEAMANS, ed., THE LEGACY OF THE DOCTRINAL TEACHINGS OF ROBERT B. THIEME, JR. (2014) (providing an excellent discussion of the grace mechanics of salvation).

[53] Olmstead v. United States, 277 U.S. 438 (1928).

[54] *Id.*

[55] *See* April White, *A Brief History of Surveillance in America*, SMITHSONIAN MAG. (Apr. 2018), https://www.smithsonianmag.com/history/brief-history-surveillance-america-180968399/.

[56] Katz v. United States, 389 U.S. 347 (1967).

intrusions on the "privacy rights" of individuals as well as to actual physical intrusions. A true originalist in 1928 would have had little trouble in extrapolating the spirit of the Fourth Amendment to modern circumstances. Obviously, when faced with new technology or factual developments which did not exist at the time the Bill of Rights was adopted—to include those created by Congress—the originalist has no problem using common sense to argue by historical analogy and reach a proper outcome completely in keeping with the spirit of the intent of the author.

For example, in *Chauffeurs, Teamsters, & Helpers, Local No. 391 v. Terry*[57] the Court had to decide whether a civil action totally unknown in 1791 was entitled to a jury trial under the provisions of the Seventh Amendment.[58] Since the Seventh Amendment only made civil actions triable to a jury at the time of the adoption of the Bill of Rights in 1791, the right to a jury trial did not include actions brought before courts of chancery (equity). Further, since modern federal pleading has combined both law and equity into a single pleading called a civil action, the courts logically adopted a "historical test"[59] to determine whether or not there is a right to a jury trial in any particular instance. If the plaintiff was entitled to a jury trial in 1791 then he would be entitled to one in 2019. While the historical test works well enough, it faces a new problem when dealing

---

[57] Chauffeurs, Teamsters, & Helpers, Local No. 391 v. Terry, 494 U.S. 558 (1990).

[58] *Id.* The Seventh Amendment provides: "In suits at common law, where the value in controversy shall exceed twenty dollars, the right of trial by jury shall be preserved, and no fact tried by a jury shall otherwise be reexamined in any Court of the United States, than according to the rules of the common law."

[59] *See* STEPHEN YEAZELL & SCHWARTZ, CIVIL PROCEDURE 617-619 (9th ed. 2016). "Presumably the drafters of the Seventh Amendment were thinking of a world in which there were separate courts of law and equity, a world in which one could only "preserve" a right to jury trial in suits at common law. Because there had never been a right to jury trial in equity, there was nothing to preserve and no right to jury trial." *Id.* at 618.

with a cause of action that was unknown to either law or equity courts in 1791. This was the dilemma in *Chauffeurs*, where the historical test was impotent. Accordingly, led by originalist thinking, the Court first unsuccessfully sought to argue by analogy to similar situations before ruling that the plaintiffs were entitled to a jury trial because the modern cause of action in question sought monetary damages, a key component of courts of law.[60]

– Originalist vs Living Constitutionalist –

As stated, the ideological battle is between the progressive living constitutionalist and the conservative originalist. The progressive is always on the attack seeking to destroy Americanism by collapsing the four establishment pillars. The originalist honors the establishment pillars and holds true to the Constitution and the words therein.

The Death Penalty –

Perhaps one of the more illustrative areas of this conflict involves the progressive's unrelenting attack upon the constitutionality of the death penalty. Amazingly, most law professors, if I had to hazard a guess, are philosophically opposed to the death penalty as a matter of "morality," but prefer to embrace a legal basis to cloak their personal feelings on the matter. Originalists support the death penalty as both moral—the Bible unequivocally endorses capital punishment—and legal per the Constitution.

Under the Eighth Amendment, individuals in America convicted of a crime have the absolute right to be free of "cruel and unusual punishment"[61] from the State. Some legal activist groups, such as the American Civil Liberties Union (ACLU), dogmatically believe that the death penalty "inherently violates the constitutional ban against cruel and

---

[60] Chauffeurs, Teamsters, & Helpers, Local No. 39, 494 U.S. at 573.

[61] U.S. CONST. amend. VIII.

unusual punishment,"[62] regardless of what the clear intent of the Framers were on the matter.   Instead of seriously exploring the original intent of the Framers, the ACLU's primary concern is over the triggering phrase "denial of civil liberties" which "is inconsistent with the fundamental values of our democratic system."[63]   Apart from the fact that the ACLU fails to understand that Americans have actually been living in a "democratic system" from the inception of the Republic and that their "fundamental values" are certainly not the same as the aforementioned pillars of fundamental values that established the nation, their opposition to the death penalty simply reflects an emotional preference undoubtedly shared by all living constitutionalists.   They merely advocate for the advancement of a strongly held belief system over the crystal-clear language of the U.S. Constitution on the matter.

Although the 1972 Supreme Court case of *Furman v. Georgia*[64] struck down the death penalty, it was only due to objections associated with how the various State death penalty laws across the nation were being applied, not to the legality of the act itself.[65]   Understanding the Court's concerns, new death penalty statutes were quickly drafted and enacted into law.   For instance, the new Georgia statute which the Court approvingly accepted in *Gregg v. Georgia*,[66] a short four years later, provided "objective standards to

---

[62]   *See The Case Against the Death Penalty,* ACLU (2012), https://www.aclu.org/other/case-against-death-penalty.

[63]   *Id.*

[64]   Furman v. Georgia, 408 U.S. 238 (1972).

[65]   *Id.* The Court referred to the application as "harsh, freakish, and arbitrary." Concurring, Justice Stewart stated: "petitioners were among a capriciously selected random handful upon whom the sentence of death was imposed, and that the Eighth and Fourteenth Amendments could not tolerate the infliction of a sentence of death under legal systems which permitted this unique penalty to be so wantonly and so freakishly imposed." *Id.*

[66]   Gregg v. Georgia, 428 U.S. 153 (1976).

guide, regularize, and make rationally reviewable the process for imposing the sentence of death."[67] Most importantly, the Court in *Gregg* clearly affirmed the constitutionality of the death penalty as a State power that "does not invariably violate the Constitution."[68] In this ruling, the originalist abides quite easily. Coupled with the fact that the death penalty existed and was in full use in 1791, is the fact that capital punishment is specifically mentioned in the U.S. Constitution as a lawful function of the State.[69] One can certainly not like the death penalty for a variety of reasons associated with a variety of rational arguments about its efficacy in stopping crime, etc., but these objections do not wash away the absolute constitutionally of the death penalty.

Accordingly, while the living constitutionalist accurately laments that the written Constitution is a giant road block to imposing progressive agendas, the truth is that the Constitution as drafted contains the means for change through the amendment process which provides a "flexible system of government with the capacity of passing laws necessary to meet the needs and challenges of contemporary America."[70] The originalist does not disavow the actual written Constitution because, within the inherent flexibility of the Constitution, there will always remain an unwavering dedication to "certain liberties deemed essential by a consensus of we the people in the several states who ratified them"[71]—the four pillars of establishment.

While the progressive advocates for a new "living Constitution" as the modern and new law of the land, the originalist embraces the actual written Constitution as the

---

[67]   *Id.*

[68]   *Id.*

[69]   *See* U.S. CONST. amend. V.

[70]   SCALIA & GARNER, *supra* note 10, at 89.

[71]   *Id.*

supreme law of the land in accordance with Article VI, clause 2:

> This Constitution, and the Laws of the United States which shall be made in pursuance thereof; and all Treaties made, or which shall be made, under the authority of the United States, shall be the supreme Law of the Land; and the judges in every State shall be bound thereby, anything in the Constitution or laws of any State to the Contrary notwithstanding.[72]

Free men and women must reject "governance by means of the decrees of an unelected body of judges"[73] dreamed up outside the parameters of the actual written Constitution. According to one commentator, this is not the rule of law; it is the rule of man.[74] If change should come to society it must be through the will of the people, not the will of five unelected Supreme Court Justices. The originalist understands his sacred obligation to protect the Constitution which in turn protects the four establishment pillars, not to alter it.

---

[72] U.S. CONST. art. VI, cl. 2.

[73] Duncan, *supra* note 9, at 20.

[74] *Id.*

Chapter Two
The Establishment Pillars

*"The trouble with man is twofold – he cannot learn
those truths that are too complex, and he forgets those
truths that are too simple."*[75]

– Rebecca West

The Bible teaches that there are three categories of Divine truth: (1) the four establishment pillars; (2) the gospel of salvation; and (3) concentrated Bible doctrine that concerns the person and work of God. Each category of Divine truth provides fantastic benefits to any human that responds positively to them in his soul.[76]

> And you will know the truth [*aletheia* (what is true in any matter under consideration)], and the truth will make you free [*eletheroo* (to set at liberty)].[77]

The first category of truth corresponds directly with the aforementioned four establishment pillars, although technically they are properly labeled as "Divine establishment pillars" due to the fact that they are directly ordained by God and revealed to mankind in the Bible. The four establishment pillars were established by God to maintain order, stability, and freedom in the human race and are meant to apply to all mankind, regardless of cultural background or religious belief system. In this context they serve as a protection from the tyranny and total depravity of

---

[75] REBECCA WEST (CICELY ISABEL FAIRFIELD), THE MEANING OF TREASON 311 (1949).

[76] *See, e.g.*, JEFFREY F. ADDICOTT, CATEGORICAL BIBLE DOCTRINES (2019).

[77] Jn. 8:32.

man, for without their restraining effect humanity would have most assuredly killed each other off a long time ago.

Again, all of humanity, regardless of cultural background or varied religious belief system, can enjoy the benefits of God's four establishment pillars. They are not for "Christians" only. In Matthew 5:24, God affirms that the establishment pillars are available for all humans.

> So that you may be sons of your Father who is in heaven; for He causes His sun to rise on the evil and the good, and sends rain on the righteous and the unrighteous.[78]

In fact, any person can enjoy great happiness in this life if he adheres to one or more of these establishment pillars. For example, in Ecclesiastes 2:24, the Bible links hard work, a vital component of establishment pillar #4, with happiness.[79]

> There is nothing better for a man than to eat and drink and tell himself that his labor [*amal*] is good. This also I [*Solomon*] have seen that it is from the hand of God.

Freedom without authority is anarchy and authority without freedom is tyranny. Thus, individuals and society alike must operate with a proper mixture of the two. As with

---

[78] Matt. 5:45.

[79] *See also,* Eccl. 9:9-10.

Enjoy [*ratsah* (to be pleased with)] life [*chay* – the unbeliever living under the umbrella of the Divine Institutions] with the woman [*ishshah* (wife; female)] whom you [the unbeliever] love [*ahab*] all the days of your fleeting [*hebel*] life [*chay*] which He [God] has given to you under the sun; for this is your reward [*cheleq* (a portion; share)] in life and in your toil [*amal* (labor)] in which you have labored under the sun. Whatever your hand finds to do, do *it* with *all* your might [*koach* (human strength)]; for there is no activity [*maaweh* (work; business)] or planning [*chashab* (to invent; to think about)] or knowledge [*daath* (premeditation; knowledge)] or wisdom [*chokmah*] in Sheol [the Lake of Fire] where you [the unbeliever] are going [*halak* (to go)].

all aspects of ordered behavior the four establishment pillars require a system of balanced and proper authority to function.

– One: Privacy/Individualism –

The emphasis under establishment pillar #1 is completely focused on the individual and his right to privacy in personal interactions. Thus, it is rooted in the individual's absolute right of self-determination. In a word, this means freedom. Recognizing that each and every human is a conscious, rational being who is uniquely different from any other person that has ever existed, or will ever exist, the focus for establishment pillar #1 is on the primacy of each and every individual to exercise free willed choices in regard to how they will live their lives. Governmental interference should be extremely limited. One thing that fundamentally rubricates Americanism is the idea that the government should: "Leave us alone."

Humans are not animals, neither are they mindless robots. They possess a real, visible material biological body and a real but immaterial soul. The soul is eternal, but the body is temporal. While the biological body has great significance, it is the soul, housed within the body, which actually constitutes the real person. As such, there are five basic characteristics of the human soul: (1) self-consciousness, the person is aware that they exist apart from every other living thing; (2) a conscience, the human being can understand the moral difference between right and wrong; (3) a super high mental capacity, used to engage in abstract thinking; (4) an emotion, used to appreciate the things around and about; and (5) a volition, the crown jewel of the soul which uniquely allows humans to make and be responsible for their free willed choices.

Human sovereignty or free will was first announced as a reality in Genesis 2:17, with God's warning to the first two humans not to eat "of the tree of the knowledge of good and evil." Both exercised their volition in a negative manner to test this concept and both chose against God's command.

Establishment pillar #1 recognizes that the right to exercise free choices within the framework of the other establishment pillars is inviolable as long as the person obeys the proper authority system that might be involved in those choices, e.g., a person cannot use their free will to commit a felony. Although an individual's right to his own privacy is the environment for true freedom, free will must function under an authority system to regulate proper outcomes.

The proper authority mechanism for establishment pillar #1 is definitely the factor of virtue. As fully discussed in Chapter 3, virtue simply matches outcome with motive—to "do a right thing in a right way." For example, it is a *right thing* to acquire money under the concept of capitalism. However, if one obtains the money by fraud then that wealth has been accumulated in a wrong way. Such a person has operated with no virtue and has done great harm to himself, his fellow man, and his nation. In other words, individuals should make free willed decisions and choices so that virtuous outcomes result. When virtue is practiced throughout the land, then prosperity booms.

The progressive ignores or flatly rejects the primacy of the individual and their free willed decisions under privacy and instead glorifies the State as the supreme authority mechanism. For them the individual's will is always subordinate to the will of the State because only the State knows best what values should be embraced or rejected. The individual is a cog in the wheel of big government and must work for the implementation of socialist agendas. Thus, it does not matter that individual rights are trampled or abrogated. People are nothing more than sacrificial animals on the altar of the greater good. All that matters for the progressive is the will and rule of the State.

– Two: Marriage –

First set out in Genesis 2:18, 24 (*see also*, 1 Cor. 7:2; Prov. 18:22), the Bible make it very clear that adult members of the opposite sex were not meant to be alone. Thus, marriage was ordained by God as the basic corporate unit for mankind and consists of a life lasting relationship between one man and one woman.[80] Even though polygamy was sometimes practiced in the Old Testament it was always against God's design as clearly outlined by Jesus in Matthew 19:3-8.

> *Some* Pharisees came to Jesus, testing Him and asking, "Is it lawful *for a man* to divorce [*apoluo* (to dismiss; to send away)] his wife for any reason at all?" And He answered and said, "Have you not read that He who created *them* from the beginning made them male and female, and said, 'For this reason a man shall leave his father and mother and be joined [*kollao* (to glue together)] to his wife, and the two shall become one flesh?' So, they are no longer two, but one flesh. What therefore God has joined together, let no man separate." They said to Him, "Why then did Moses command to give her a certificate of divorce and send *her* away?" He said to them, "Because of your hardness of heart Moses

---

[80] *See e.g.,* Rom. 1:26-27.

For this reason God gave them over to degrading [*atimia*] passions [*pathos* (an affliction of the mind)]; for their women exchanged the natural [*phusikos* (produced by nature)] function [*chresis* (of the sexual use of a woman)] for that which is unnatural [*phusis* (perverse; abnormal)], and in the same way also the men abandoned [*aphiemi* (to send away)] the natural function of the woman and burned [*ekkaio* (to set on fire)] in their desire [*orexis*] toward one another [*allelon* (one another of the same kind)], men with men committing [*katergazomai* (to perform)] indecent acts and receiving [*apolambano*] in their own persons the due penalty of their error.

permitted you to divorce your wives; but from the beginning it has not been this way."[81]

While non-married single adults have complete independence and sovereignty over their individual lives, marriage is a full working partnership requiring a maximum amount of virtue from each partner. Interestingly, although the man was designated by God as the senior partner in this relationship, in exercising his role as husband the man is commanded to elevate his wife to a superior position to himself in terms of love, provision, and care. For the Christian, the husband is commanded to love his wife as his own body and further, to love her as Christ loved the Church. Respectively, Ephesians 5:25, 28 states:

> Husbands, love your wives, just as Christ also loved the church and gave Himself up for her [Jesus Christ suffered spiritual death on the cross in order to provide salvation].[82]

> So husbands ought also to love their own wives as their own bodies. He who loves his own wife loves himself.[83]

A rather precise series of instructions on marriage is expounded on throughout the Bible and a variety of important points can be gleaned to advance the concept. First, marriage is not a "religious" function per se as it is a relationship that is designed to produce stability in society, not religious dogma. Second, the married couple is to subordinate all other human relationships and interactions to the marriage, to include the strongest pre-marital relationship of parents. The marriage relationship is now supreme as set out in Genesis 2:24-25.

> For this reason a man shall leave [azab (to depart from)] his father and his mother, and be joined [dabaq (to join to)] to his wife; and they shall become

---

[81]   Matt. 19:3-8.

[82]   Eph. 5:25.

[83]   Eph. 5:28.

one flesh [this was a prediction]. And the man and his wife were both naked [*arom*] and were not ashamed [*bush* (to feel shame) – prior to the Fall].[84]

Third, marriage is also the sanctification of male/female love. Many passages speak about the "love bond" and include Hebrews 13:4; 1 Thessalonians 4:2-4; and Mark 10:6-9. Both partners are to remain socially and sexually faithful to one another. The sin of adultery, one of the Ten Commandments, is prohibited. 1 Thessalonians 4:2-4:

> For you know what commandments [*paraggelia* (a command)] we [Paul and his team] gave you by *the authority of* the Lord Jesus. For this is the will of God, your sanctification; *that is*, that you abstain [*apecho* (to hold back)] from sexual immorality [*porneia* (illicit sexual intercourse)]; that each of you know how to possess [*ktaomai* (to marry a wife)] his own vessel [*skeuos*] in sanctification and honor [*time*].[85]

Fourth, selecting a life-long partner is one of the most critical decisions that a person will make. It can be the source of great happiness according to Proverbs 18:22:

> He who finds a wife [*ishshah*] finds a good thing and obtains favor from the Lord.[86]

Marriage can also be the source of great unhappiness—hell on earth. Tragically, many people marry for the wrong reasons to include matters related to sex, status, or security. Selecting the right reason to marry requires a complete understanding of what marriage is designed to provide and what it is not designed to provide. In this light, there is really no benefit in meeting a proper mate if one has no capacity to enjoy them in the marriage environment. Capacity to enjoy the institution of marriage comes through learning about how it is meant to operate. In short, it is not about meeting

---

[84]   Gen. 2:24-25.

[85]   1 Thess. 4:2-4.

[86]   Prov. 18:22.

the "right" person, it is really about being the "right" person – someone who understands the value and significance of all the establishment pillars.

Even without fully comprehending the significance of marriage and the roles for each person in the relationship, common sense would dictate that a single person would be wise to stay clear of a jealous person, a compulsive gambler, a drunk, an irrational person, a gossip, or a violent tempered person. In addition, a Christian single is commanded not to marry a non-Christian per 2 Corinthians 6:14, although if a Christian does marry a non-Christian they are to stay as they are in the marriage and not seek divorce.

In dating, the Bible also repeatedly commands one to abstain from sexual relations as each is someone's future husband or wife. Indeed, apart from all the other reasons that might be listed for abstaining from pre-marital sex, unchecked fornication has the potential to destroy one's mental "capacity" to enjoy a healthy sexual relationship in marriage. Accordingly, both parties in dating should not engage in activities that unduly arouse sexuality per 1 Corinthians 7:9.

> But if they [male and female Believers in dating] do not have self-control [*egkrateuomai* (to be self-controlled)], let them marry [*gameo*]; for it is better to marry than to burn [*puroo* (to burn with fire)] *with passion.*[87]

Fornication is a cheap substitute in order to gratify a biological or emotional urge. Because it can destroy the capacity to enjoy sex and rapport with one's future mate, the Christian is commanded to "flee fornication" which means to avoid this particular sin. 1 Corinthians 6:18:

> Flee [*pheugo* (to run away quickly)] immorality [*porneia* (illicit sexual intercourse)]. Every other sin [*hamartema*] that a man commits [*poieo* (to do)] is outside the body [*soma*], but the immoral [*porneuo*

---

[87] 1 Cor. 7:9. *See also* 2 Tim. 2:22.

(to prostitute one's body to the lust of another)] man sins against his own body [the capacity for true love is denigrated].[88]

In the dating process, there are three stages of social contact between dating couples and the wise single is careful in each stage before marriage: (1) attraction; (2) compatibility; and (3) rapport.

Attraction. A great many single members of the opposite sex may fall into this category as attraction is based on a wide variety of factors ranging from physical attraction to mental attraction. In this stage of dating, one should closely observe how the date treats other people, particularly those who can do nothing for them, as a person's attitude towards other people is a barometer on their capacity to love. For the wise, this initial stage of the dating "two-step" is generally short in duration—losers are everywhere.

Compatibility. The compatibility stage is where the dating partners clearly ascertain compatible norms and standards, likes and dislikes. This stage generally takes some time to fully determine.

Rapport. This is the final stage which precedes actual marriage and is rarely achieved without both parties well versed in the faults of the other and yet "in love" with that person. The word "love" is now meaningfully employed— it emanates from the free will of each and is freely given. Most importantly, both realize that their soul is aroused by the other as expressed in Song of Solomon 8:6-7.

> Put me [a man telling his girlfriend] like a seal [*chotham* (a signet ring worn on a woman's necklace)] over your heart [*leb*], like a seal on your arm. For love is as strong as death, jealousy [*qinah* (to burn up)] is as severe as Sheol; its flashes [*respeph* (flame)] are flashes of fire, the *very* flame of the Lord. Many waters [pressures and problems] cannot quench love, nor will rivers overflow it; if a

---

[88] 1 Cor. 6:18.

man were to give all the riches of his house for love, it would be utterly despised.[89]

By saying "I do," in the actual marriage ceremony, both agree to surrender their independence and freedom in order to obtain something better—the partnership of marriage.[90] The benefits of marriage include the following: (a) norms and standards in the soul of each match and find fulfillment; (b) reality is given to romantic dreams; (c) a powerful fragrance of memory is developed; and (d) soul stimulation is obtained, as all good sex comes from concentration. Indeed, in sexual relations in marriage there is no authority designated between the husband and wife—each may initiate and respond in sex. The husband must not demand sex, but the wife should not refuse sex. Exceptions to suspending the "love life" are to be for short periods of time per 1 Corinthians 7:5.

> The wife does not have authority over [*exousiazo* (to have full and entire authority over the body)] her own body [*soma*], but the husband *does*; and likewise also the husband [*aner*] does not have authority over [*exousiazo*] his own body, but the wife does. Stop depriving [*apostereo*] one another [of sex], except by agreement for a time, so that you may devote yourselves to prayer, and come together again [in sex] so that Satan will not tempt [*peirazo* (to test)] you because of your lack of self-control.[91]

Finally, the Bible has much to say about problems in marriage and their solutions. The unhappily married mate may seek satisfaction/stimulation by social unfaithfulness, substitution, or sublimation. Problems can emerge from the

---

[89] S. S. 8:6-7.

[90] *See* Eph. 5:22-23.

Wives, *be subject* to your own husbands [*aner*], as to the Lord. For the husband is the head [*kephale*] of the wife, as Christ also is the head of the church [*ekklesia*], He Himself *being* the Savior of the body.

[91] 1 Cor. 7:4-5.

following general categories: (a) personality differences; (b) jealousy; (c) legalism, which includes moral self-righteousness; (d) unfaithfulness or immoral degeneracy, where one seeks the company of others—either sexual or social; (e) lack of communication and concentration; (f) lack of reciprocation; and (g) the departure of initial attractiveness.

Solutions to marital problems range from properly learning (or relearning) how to perform the requirements of a husband or wife, as the case may be, to the ultimate problem solving device which is set out in Ephesians 4:32—forget any real or imagined wrongs and forgive your spouse:

> Be kind [*chrestos* (virtuous; benevolent)] to one another, tender-hearted [*eusplagchnos* (compassionate)], forgiving each other, just as God in Christ also has forgiven you [no believer in Christ deserved salvation].[92]

Apart from recognizing the critical requirement of patience and forgiveness in the marriage relationship, both the woman and the man must be taught how to properly fulfill their respective roles in marriage. While the Bible reveals the existence of differences in terms of how males and females are genetically "wired" and physically built—the female is a responder to her husband per Genesis 3:16 and the male is the initiator—learning how to effectively function in a marriage requires a fair amount of learning. As previously noted, the husband must be taught to place his wife above himself which goes hand in hand with true leadership. As it applies to the female, Titus 2:3-5 encourages older married ladies to assist in this task.

> Older women likewise are to be reverent in their behavior, not malicious gossips [*diabolos* (prone to slander)] nor enslaved to much wine, teaching what is good [*kalodidaskalos* (a teacher of good things)], so that they may encourage the young women to love

---

[92] Eph. 4:32.

their husbands, to love their children, *to be* sensible [*sophron* (of sound mind)], pure [*hagnos* (chaste; modest)], workers at home [*oikouros* (keeper of the house)], kind, being subject to their own husbands, so that the word of God will not be dishonored.[93]

A wife and husband who learn and understand the benefits of the marriage relationship are not only a blessing to one another but to the entire community in which they reside. In Proverbs 31:10-31, the Bible describes what can only be categorized as the "super wife." Given that women in or out of marriage are fully entitled and capable of performing management positions at any level in business, this particular wife is described as a successful business executive in the private sector, community leader, wonderful mother to her children, and fantastic lover!

– Racism, Sexism, & Other Phobias, Oh My!

The progressive flatly rejects the Biblical view of marriage and employs every "ism" in the book to slander and malign it. Not only is it unthinkable that so-called absolute "equality" between the two sexes is not the Biblical standard for the marriage relationship, but progressives substitute any number of alternative pairings between people to qualify as a legitimate "marriage," to include same sex partners.

Apart from enduring ridicule and scorn for holding such outdated Biblical views on marriage, some conservatives have actually been subjected to legal sanctions for not towing the new Supreme Court line on the matter.[94] One

---

[93] Tit. 2:3-5. *See also*, 1 Pet. 3:1-2.

[94] *See* Jonathan Zimmerman, *God Once Opposed Interracial Marriage, Too*, PITTSBURGH POST-GAZETTE (Mar. 9, 2019), https://www.post-gazette.com/opinion/Op-Ed/2019/03/10/God-once-opposed-interracial-marriage-too/stories/201903070010 (suggesting that the United Methodist Church is on "the wrong side of history. . . ."); Michael Foust, *Christian Photographer Fights Law that Could Force Her to Promote Same-Sex Weddings*, CHRISTIAN HEADLINES (Nov. 25, 2019), https://www.christianheadlines.com/contributors/michael-foust/christian-photographer-fights-law-that-could-force-her-to-promote-

thing is clear, both views cannot be correct—either the Bible is correct about marriage or the progressive is correct. Again, the breathtaking progressive victory regarding what consists marriage was achieved not by any piece of legislation at the State or federal level but by means of a single Supreme Court case which split 5-4, rendered in 2015.[95]

– Three: Family –

Beginning in Genesis 4, the nuclear family is designated as the proper place to teach and instruct children. Since, babies are born absolutely helpless and must rely on the care and nurturing of their parents for survival, it is only natural that the parents should have the primary responsibility to raise them and to teach them to respect the establishment pillars.

The fifth commandment in the Old Testament's Ten Commandments requires the offspring to honor their parents. It also provides a promise to those that do so.

Honor your father and your mother, that your days may be prolonged in the land which the Lord your God gives to you.[96]

In the New Testament's Ephesians 6:1-3, the Bible makes it clear that this promise of a long life applies not just

---

same-sex-weddings.html (providing an example of a Kentucky law that will force a Christian photographer to violate her religious beliefs and her First Amendment rights); Diana Chandler, *Biblical Marriage, Gender Views Cited in 2 Ousters* (July 15, 2019), http://www.bpnews.net/53281/biblical-marriage-gender-views-cited-in-2-ousters ("A Southern Baptist church employee in Texas and a Maryland Christian school have been dropped from public programs, accused of discrimination for promoting Bible-based views of marriage and gender.").

[95] Obergefell v. Hodges, 135 S. Ct. 2584 (2015) (finding a fundamental right to marry for same sex couples).

[96] Ex. 20:12.

to the Old Testament Jews. The obligation to respect and honor parents starts in the home but extends throughout life.

> Children, obey your parents in the Lord, for this is right. Honor your father and your mother (which is the first commandment with a promise), so that it may be well with you, and that you may live long on the earth.[97]

Furthermore, as long as the child resides in the home of the parents, the authority system resides with both of the parents. Colossians 3:20 states:

> Children, be obedient to your parents in all things, for this is well-pleasing to the Lord.[98]

Finally, the Bible cautions parents to use their authority over their minor children in fairness and love. This does not mean that parents can shun their responsibility to discipline their children. In fact, parents who refuse to discipline their children are creating societal monsters. While spanking should be limited to a narrow window during say early pre-school up to perhaps early elementary school, other forms of discipline may be employed into the teenage years. Proverbs 13:24 makes this point very clear.

> He who withholds his rod hates his son, but he who loves him disciplines him diligently.[99]

However, all parental discipline—to include corporal punishment—must be preceded by a "trial" and that discipline must be appropriate and never abusive (punching or slapping the child's face is abuse). Brutality only produces resentment and anger in the child. Although Ephesians 6:4 is a command to the father towards the minor child in this regard, both the father and the mother are authorized to discipline and instruct the child. In fact, in the

---

[97] Eph. 6:1-3.

[98] Col. 3:20.

[99] Prov. 13:24.

American South, it is generally the mother that performs corporal punishment on the minor children.

> Fathers, do not provoke your children to anger, but bring them up in the discipline and instruction of the Lord.[100]

– They Are Coming for Your Kids

Understanding the importance of bending young minds to their way of thinking, progressives are extremely active in finding new mechanisms to usurp the authority of parents. Under socialism, children are viewed as the "property" of the State, not the parent. Controlled by progressives, the State tells the child what to think and what to believe. While children are not carted off to "education" camps in America just yet, the progressive long ago found a way to brainwash them anyway. This feat is accomplished with amazing success through the various State and federal public educational systems which unilaterally decree where the child shall go to school and what the child shall learn in school.

Tragically, in our educational system progressive ideology is keen to engage in fake history and even "false history."[101] On the one hand they attack the Founding Fathers with great opprobrium because of their devotion to the four establishment pillars, while simultaneously seeking to recast them into early champions of progressivism. Amazingly, a core false narrative in our educational system is that living constitutionalist thinking has always been the mainstream in American thinking—at least amongst the "intelligent class." This outrageous idea is not just relegated to the mantra of large portions of academia, adherents

---

[100] Eph. 6:4.

[101] *See* William Jeynes, "Fake History" is More Dangerous Than "Fake News", PUBLIC DISCOURSE: THE JOURNAL OF THE WITHERSPOON INSTITUTE (May 15, 2017), https://www.thepublicdiscourse.com/2017/05/19322/.

tirelessly work to insert it into the very historical record of the nation.

For instance, if one visits the official public museum located in the basement of the fabulous Jefferson Memorial in Washington, D.C., there is a large colored wall-display depicting a sitting female with an American flag and a Greek goddess with outstretched hand standing to her right, as if instructing the sitting female figure. It is obvious that the Greek goddess represents the enlightened voice of "progressive change" and the sitting figure represents America. To ensure that this symbol is properly interpreted, above the drawing there is a partial quote from President Thomas Jefferson. The quote is set out in very large font. It reads as follows:

> Laws and institutions must go hand in hand with the progress of the human mind. As that becomes more developed, more enlightened, as new discoveries are made, new truths disclosed, and manners and opinions change with the change of circumstances, institutions must advance also, and keep pace with the times. Thomas Jefferson, 1816.[102]

Of course, to the serious student of American history this display at Jefferson's Memorial is an outrage. It is a perfect example of fake history. In order to foist the views of the living constitutionalist on an unsuspecting public, the words of Jefferson are grossly taken out of context. Indeed, given that the full quotation would actually support originalism, not living constitutionalism, some unprincipled individual(s) employed by our own federal government intentionally deleted the first sentence of Jefferson's famous remark. That first sentence which rubricates all that follows says: "I am certainly not an advocate for frequent and untried changes in laws and Constitutions. But laws and institutions. . . ."[103] In

---

[102] The display is in the small museum, under the Jefferson Memorial, detailing Thomas Jefferson's life and beliefs.

[103] Letter from Thomas Jefferson to Samuel Kercheval (Jul. 12, 1816) (on file with the National Archives: Founders Online,

addition, the person who crafted the so-called quote at the museum display also intentionally chose not to put brackets around the first word in their display quote which is "Laws." Thus, their Jefferson quote should have started as: "[L]aws. . . ." Proper English grammar mandates the placing of a bracket around the "L" which would at least alert the reader that the display's creator had broken into the Jefferson full sentence for their selected quote, prompting the inquisitive to look up the full quote to see what preceded the word "laws."

In tandem with the matter of public propaganda, so-called community experts, who increasingly fall into the progressive camp of thinking, have great influence on setting educational curriculum. To those that can still think for themselves, it is shockingly apparent that large swaths of the academic curriculum in many school systems at all grade levels is carefully scripted to ignore or openly denigrate the sacred principles of the establishment pillars. Indeed, progressives are no longer content to simply bypass the establishment pillars, they now use the educational process to openly mock patriotism, capitalism, nationalism, marriage, respect for law enforcement, the military, etc.

The only solution to counter the markedly anti-establishment propaganda oozing out of today's educational systems is for the parent to carefully monitor what the public schools are doing and to teach their children in the home about the beauty and benefit of the establishment pillars. With rare exceptions, the schools are anti-establishment pillars.

If parents refuse this responsibility, little Suzy or little Johnny won't have a chance to resist the group think of most educational systems when they march off to college dorms. They will be easy prey for progressive recruitment and hardly recognizable within a year's time. In a sense, parents must immunize their children from progressivism during the

http://www.let.rug.nl/usa/presidents/thomas-jefferson/letters-of-thomas-jefferson/jefl246.php.

child's formative years, and in some cases even actively "deprogram" them. Only then can the child have a fighting chance to survive the assorted evils of modern education when it comes to rationally viewing the establishment pillars.

– Four: Nationalism –

Establishment pillar #4 is clearly found throughout the Bible, running from such passages as Genesis 10:5, 32 and Deuteronomy 32:8 in the Old Testament to Acts 17:26-28, 1 Peter 2:13-18, and Colossians 1:16 in the New Testament. Nationalism refers to the functions of a proper Bible-based governmental structure that protects all forms of individual freedom and the basic human rights of its citizens who reside in a national entity—what is called in modern terminology the nation/state. While nationalism is the proper framework in which the inalienable right of the individual to acquire and own private property under capitalism operates, it also embraces other collateral truths. The authority resides with the State and its supporting apparatus operating under a just rule of law carried out by domestic law enforcement and virtuous judges on the bench. In turn, directly associated with nationalism are a series of additional and vital support components briefly outlined below.

– Limited Government

The first component of nationalism is the requirement for the central government to be limited. America was founded directly on this principle of limited government power. Understanding Lord Acton's observation that centralized power tends to corrupt and absolute power corrupts absolutely,[104] the freedom oriented nation will always reject centralization of power to include internationalism—the alter that all progressives worship at—and endorse a system

---

[104] Letter from Lord Acton to Bishop Creighton (1887)(https://oll.libertyfund.org/quotes/214).

of limited government with maximum power given to the people and local government. In America, the States came together to form a single nation, but only when guaranteed the rights of autonomy set out in the Bill of Rights. The new nation provided for limited government only, while leaving the citizens at liberty to pursue their own desires as individuals through free associations and free enterprise. In short, big government makes little people. Little government makes big people.

Internationalism seeks to consolidate all power into one massive organization, while nationalism works to oppose this. As such nationalism is the only way to guarantee that human freedom will exist somewhere in the world. To illustrate the concept from the Biblical viewpoint, the first attempt by humans to set up "internationalism" was the Tower of Babel episode. God is a nationalist. God struck it down in Genesis 11:1-9.

– Capitalism

Second, along with the restriction on the government's involvement in the daily lives of its people rests a guarantee for them to earn and keep their own money—to fully engage in laissez faire capitalism. In the main this means a policy or attitude of simply letting things take their own path with minimal interference from the government. This is part of the American dream which proclaims that success waits on the far side of hard work.

Money is a necessity of life and necessary for the proper operation of the economy—it is not wrong as the progressive asserts for individuals to make and keep money.[105] The Bible only condemns the love of money as a great evil, not money in and of itself. Most certainly, the lust for money is wrong and is a dead end for those who seek happiness in the accumulation of wealth to the exclusion of all else. This truism is set out in 1 Timothy 6:10.

---

[105] Gen. 23:9; Jer. 32:44.

> For the love of money [*philarguria* (love of money; avarice)] is a root [*rhiza* (that which springs from a root)] of all sorts of evil [*kakos*], and some by longing [*oregomai* (to stretch one's self out in order to touch something)] for it have wandered away [*apoplanao* (to cause to go astray)] from the faith [*pisits* – learning Bible doctrine] and pierced [*peripeiro* (to pierce through)] themselves with many griefs [*odune* (a consuming grief or pain) – self-induced misery].[106]

The same point is made in Hebrews 13:5-6.

> Make sure that your character [*tropos* (a manner of life)] is free from the love of money [*aphilarguros* (not loving money; not avaricious)], being content [*arkeo* (to be satisfied)] with what you have; for He Himself has said, "I will never desert you, nor will I ever forsake you," so that we confidently [*tharrheo* (to be of good courage)] say, "The Lord is my helper, I will not be afraid [*phobeo*]. What will man do to me?"[107]

In Mark 8:36-37, the Bible compares the acquisition of money to the ultimate issue in life—money will not provide salvation. Money can do many things in this temporal life, but it must always be put into its proper perspective.

> For what does it profit a man to gain [*kerdaino* (to gain; to acquire)] the whole world [*kosmos*], and forfeit [*zemioo* (to suffer loss)] his soul [*psuche*]? For what will a man give in exchange [*antallagma* (that which is given in place of another)] for his soul?[108]

---

[106] 1 Tim. 6:10. *See also* Heb. 13:5; Phil. 4:11.

[107] Heb. 13:5-6. *See also*, Ps. 11:72:

The law [*tora* – the Bible] of Your mouth is better [*tob*] to me than thousands of gold and silver *pieces*.

[108] Mk. 8:36-37. *See also*, Lk. 12:19-21:

Thus, the proper national entity must provide a system of free enterprise so that people can advance and prosper under their own free entrepreneurial decisions. Again, nationalism coupled with capitalism fragments the consolidation and centralization of governmental power. Centralized governmental power cannot create wealth and in reality always stifles free thinking, innovation, and economic growth. The freedom-oriented nation recognizes the right of private ownership of property and the right to conduct business apart from undue interference from the State.

The dual Biblical commands embracing capitalism are set out early in the Ten Commandments at Exodus 20:15, 17. God makes it very clear in terms of private ownership of property: Thou shalt not steal," and "Thou shalt not covet." With the first commandment, God endorses the private ownership of property. In turn, the companion commandment makes it a sin to lust after the private property of another. While a central ingredient of socialism is based on covetousness—the lust for taking the property of another under the guise that it is "unfair" that they should have it while another does not—the freedom oriented nation recognizes that capitalism will produce some level of poverty, but far greater levels of opportunity. Socialism inevitably leads to levels of great poverty and no opportunity. Exodus 20:17:

> You shall not covet your neighbor's [*rea* (fellow-citizen)] house; you shall not covet your neighbor's wife or his male servant or his female

---

And I will say to my soul [*psuche*], "Soul, you have many goods laid up for many years *to come*; take your ease, eat, drink *and* be merry." But God said to him, "'You fool [*aphron* (one without reason)]! This *very* night your soul [*psuche*] is required [*apaiteo* (to demand back)] – at physical death the immaterial soul departs the material body] of you; and *now* who will own what you have prepared?' So is the man who stores up treasure for himself, and is not rich [*plouteo* – the ultimate wealth is possessing the Righteousness of God for salvation] toward God."

servant or his ox or his donkey or anything that belongs to your neighbor.[109]

Ironically, the true measure of capitalism is not necessarily "look at our prosperity" but "look at our freedom and opportunity." Of course, capitalism requires a strong work ethic which is mandated in the Bible for all members of society. In short, all able-bodied adults must "get a job."[110] The Bible commands that one should work for a living. In 2 Thessalonians 3:10-12, Paul writes:

> For even when we were with you [Paul and his traveling seminary team], we used to give you this order: if anyone is not willing to work [*ergazomai* (to labor; to do work)], then he is not to eat, either. For we hear that some among you are leading an undisciplined life, doing no work at all, but acting like busybodies [*periergazomai* (to bustle about uselessly)]. Now such persons we command and exhort [*parakaleo* (to address forcefully)] in the Lord Jesus Christ to work [*ergazomai* – get a job] in quiet fashion [*hesuchia* (quietness; does not meddle with the affairs of others)] and eat their own bread.[111]

Capitalism may suffer from the dishonesty of either management or workers who refuse to act with virtue, but

---

[109] Ex. 20:17.

[110] The false notion that Christianity endorses socialism and not capitalism is based on Acts 2:43-47. This passage describes joint sharing of property in the early Christian Church in Jerusalem. This was the exception to the general rule and addressed an immediate problem faced by the new Jewish believers in Christ. All of them were excommunicated from the Jewish Temple and synagogues so that they were forced to pool their assets in order to survive – Acts 2:43-47. No one would buy from their businesses and no one would sell them goods and services. Thus, the only monetary collection that was taken up by Paul was for the relief of the Jewish believers in Jerusalem – 1 Cor. 16:1-4; 2 Cor. 8:1-9; Rom. 15:14-32; Acts 24:17. All other believers in every other Church were instructed to work with their own hands.

[111] 2 Thess. 3:10-12. *See also* 1 Thess. 4:11; Prov. 13:11.

socialism is inherently evil. There is never a time when it is a good. Proverbs 13:11 says:

Wealth obtained by fraud dwindles, but the one who gathers by labor increases it.[112]

– Taxes

Third, there must be a fair system of taxation. The government needs money to operate and it obtains the majority of that money by taxing its people. Taxation is a critical component of nationalism, but the amount must be fair and just. Over taxation leads to great consternation to a free people as illustrated by the early complaints from the Colonial Americans which ultimately led them to secede from Great Britain in 1776. Interestingly, over taxation was also the key reason that the first Jewish nation divided into two separate kingdoms in 930 B.C., when Solomon's successor and son, Rehoboam, increased taxes. The Southern Kingdom called Judah remained loyal to the new King, but the Northern Kingdom called Israel broke away.

Given their relationship with British rule, the Founding Fathers understood the need for a fair tax system. They also knew the Bible's position on the matter of what constitutes a just and fair tax. The Bible endorses a fixed percentage of income tax for each person regardless of social or economic status. In the Old Testament this tax was known as the "tithe" and was different from the concept of "offerings" also set out in the Bible.

Israel began as a Theocracy circa 1450 B.C. and later a Monarchy circa 1,000 B.C., based on fixed legal principles and a spiritual heritage set out in the Mosaic Law. In the several Jewish national entities of the Old Testament there was a distinction between the required tax on every citizen called "tithing" and grace giving to the Temple called "offerings."[113] The offerings were deposited by the

---

[112]   Prov. 13:11.

[113]   *See* Mk. 12:41-44:

individual in a special box placed in the outer Temple,[114] the tithings were collected by tax collectors. The distinction between the two is set out in Malachi 3:8-10.

> Will a man rob [*qaba*] God? Yet you [Jewish citizens] are robbing Me [God]! But you say, "How have we robbed You?" In tithes [*maawer* (the tenth part)] and offerings [*terumah* (any contribution)]. You are cursed with a curse, for you are robbing Me, the whole nation *of you*! Bring the whole tithe into the storehouse [the treasury], so that there may be food in My house, and test Me now in this, says the Lord of hosts, if I will not open for you the windows of heaven and pour out for you a blessing until it overflows.[115]

So, while there was never a fixed amount mandated for an individual who wanted to give in terms of "offerings" to the Temple, the tithe was always a fixed percentage of personal income and required from every adult person in the nation. The tithe was tantamount to our modern-day income tax. Curiously, however, the Old Testament tithing was not a graduated tax system (the higher the income the more the tax).[116] Many economists argue that a graduated tax system

---

> And He [Jesus] sat down opposite the treasury [*gazophulakion* (a public repository of money)], and *began* observing how the people were putting money [*chalkos* (metallic coins)] into the treasury; and many rich people were putting in large sums. A poor widow came and put in two small copper coins, which amount to a cent [*kodrantes* (a fourth part of a coin)]. Calling His disciples to Him, He said to them, "Truly I say to you, this poor widow put in more than all the contributors to the treasury; for they all put in out of their surplus, but she, out of her poverty, put in all she owned, all she had to live on."

[114] *See* Lk. 21:1-4.

[115] Mal. 3:8-10. *See also* Ex. 25:1-2.

[116] When added up, the tithing types in the Old Testament could amount to quite a hefty cut of personal income, particularly when other man-made taxes were also collected to include the Greeks and Romans when in control of the Jewish State:

tends to destroy free enterprise and is an invasion of personal privacy to boot!

– The Military

Fourth, the overt protection of the nation on exterior lines is the function of a large, strong and disciplined armed force which produces military victory on the battlefield when so required (1 Samuel 17:1-58), or deterrence. The armed force is a sharp saber and its primary mission is to protect the nation from any threat to its people or interests. This does not necessarily require the use of the saber in every instance of national security concern, but it does require that the saber be a large one so that deterrence can operate. In fact, rattling

---

(a) A 10% tax on all the Jews to support the tribe of the Levites – Numbers 18:20-21; Deuteronomy 12:17-19. The Levites were obligated to provide religious instruction and perform the rituals per the Mosaic Law.

(b) Another 10% for various sacrifices – Deuteronomy 14:22-27; Hebrews 7:5, 9.

(c) Another 10% every third year for the poor – Deuteronomy 14:28-29. It is well worth noting that this State welfare was limited with the expectation that all able-bodied people seek employment.

(d) The monarchy and government also took a percentage – Matthew 17:24-27. The tax imposed by the political ruler was 10% on land valuation and 10% on personal property – 1 Samuel 8:15, 17.

(e) All references to tithing condemn legalism – Luke 11:42; Matthew 23:23, 26.

> Woe to you, scribes and Pharisees [recruited from the scribes/lawyers], hypocrites [*hupokrites*]! For you tithe [*apodekatoo* (to exact a tenth)] mint [*heduosmon* (a sweet smelling mint)] and dill [*anethon*] and cummin [*kuminon* (a cultivated plant used for medicinal purposes)], and have neglected the weightier provisions [*barus* (heavy in weight)] of the law [the Mosaic law]: justice [*krisis*] and mercy [*eleos*] and faithfulness [*pistis*]; but these are the things you should have done without neglecting the others [these Jewish leaders and judges should have judged rightly and impartially under establishment pillar #4].

the saber is often all that is required to avert war. Of course, if the saber is the size of a McDonald's plastic knife it will not deter aggressive acts from foreign enemies. More than any other factor, it is the military that guarantees the survival of the nation. The American fighting soldier in uniform is the symbol of our freedom, not "old glory."

Accordingly, patriotism in the citizenry—people willing to fight and die for their country—must be encouraged and instilled in the young so that the national entity can raise and maintain a vibrant and respected military that operates under civilian control. The United States has built the largest and most robust military in the modern world. There is simply no question that this factor has contributed greatly to world peace and national stability. When unleased it is devastating and even in its sheath it is a powerful deterrent to aggressive nations across the globe. Conversely, a small and weak military only invites warfare.

Progressives understand the need for military force but because of their commitment to destroy the establishment pillars they seek to demoralize or downgrade the institution. Seldom do they praise the prowess of American military might as a force for good in the world, but rather as a tool of imperialism.

– Law Enforcement and Civil Justice

Fifth, the nation must have a strong domestic police force operating under a just judicial system that does not coddle criminal behavior but ensures due process and equal justice under the law for those accused of wrongdoing. Interior protection of freedom requires law and order by the police and proper jurisprudence by the courts. Accordingly, as previously discussed, capital punishment is authorized in the Bible. In 1 Peter 2:13-14 the Christian is commanded to respect law and order.

> Submit [*hupotasso*] yourselves for the Lord's sake to every human institution, whether to a king as the one in authority, or to governors as sent by him [the one

in authority] for the punishment [*ekdikesis* (criminal justice)] of evildoers and the praise of those who do right.[117]

The judicial system in an establishment-oriented nation does not primarily make laws to solve social problems in society, but to protect the freedom and privacy of its people. Indeed, the Bible is very lucid on the matter—social problems such as poverty will always exist. For instance, Jesus himself noted that "the poor you will have with you always."[118] Criminal and civil laws for society should be made on the basis of the best interests of the majority. In fact, all laws should be made for the general principle only, not the myriad exceptions to the general rule.

– Religious Freedom

Sixth, the nation must promote religious freedom for its people. Freedom of religion, however, does not mean freedom from religion. The national government resting on establishment pillars recognizes and embraces a firm belief in God, they simply don't force their citizens to do the same. People should be absolutely free to adopt any system of belief as long as it functions within the parameters of the criminal code and does not conflict with the freedoms guaranteed by the Constitution and Bill of Rights. Indeed, many of the first Europeans came to America because of religious persecution.[119] Jesus made this distinction in Matthew 19:20-21.

---

[117] 1 Pet. 2:13-14.

[118] Matt. 26:11; Mark 14:7.

[119] The Christian is commanded to be tolerate of other religious beliefs and to live in obedience to lawful governmental authority. The only exception is when that government command directly conflicts with certain aspects of Christian belief – 1 Pet. 2:13-14; Acts 4:18-20; Dan. 3:16-19; 6:10. In Acts 4:18-20 Peter and John responded as follows:

> And when they [the Jewish High Council] had summoned them [Peter and John], they commanded them not to speak [*phtheggomai* (to give out a sound)] or teach [*didasko* (to hold

"Show Me [Jesus] the coin *used* for the poll-tax." And they [Pharisees], brought Him a denarius. And He said to them, "Whose likeness and inscription is this?" They said to Him, "Caesar's." Then He said to them, "Then render to Caesar the things that are Caesar's; and to God the things that are God's."[120]

---

discourse)] at all in the name of Jesus. But Peter and John answered and said to them, "Whether it is right in the sight of God to give heed to you rather than to God, you be the judge; for we cannot stop speaking about what we have seen [*horao* (a panoramic view)] and heard [Jesus Christ's in a resurrection body]."

[120] Matt. 22:19-21.

Chapter Three

When Good is "No Good"

"Who unto them that call evil good, and good evil."

– Isaiah 5:20a

Great nations are neither created, nor sustained by accident. To a large degree, great nations are maintained by people who understand, and then are able to apply, fundamental establishment principles which provide for individual liberty. The unparalleled prosperity and freedom enjoyed by Americans over the past 200 plus years is no accident. In large part it is based on the purposeful adoption of certain bedrock principles of conduct which the Founding Fathers took from the Judeo/Christian Bible and institutionalized into the fabric of government via the Declaration of Independence, the Constitution, and the Bill of Rights. At the inception of the Republic, the early Americans had a strong rooting in these values and it took little effort to convince them that these fixed principles— previously identified as the four pillars of establishment— were both reasonable and valid constructs for ordering the workings of the country. To echo the creation story in Genesis, these principles of order and behavior were "very good." In fact, they constitute the true standard by which to measure individual and national morality.

While subsequent generations of Americans have generally exhibited the moral and religious-based values required to maintain the integrity of those principles—both institutionalized in law and in society—the beginning of the twenty-first century has witnessed an open rebellion by certain radicalized segments of the population to completely denigrate and destroy them. Again, whether they call themselves progressives, secularists, socialists, or even communists they are intent on destroying the establishment pillars and anyone who has the courage to publicly support those pillars. In a speech given at Notre Dame Law School in October 2019, Attorney General William Barr identified those most responsible for the assault on what he termed our traditional values, i.e., the four establishment pillars. He stated:

> Secularists, and their allies among the "progressives," have marshalled all the force of mass communications, popular culture, the entertainment industry, and academia in an unremitting assault on religion and *traditional values* [emphasis added].[121]

It is a simple fact of our times that what the progressives cannot accomplish by intimidation and propaganda, they seek to achieve by manipulation of the Constitution and the law. Attorney General Barr went on to lament the way that the living constitutionalist and his allies use the courts "as a battering ram to break down traditional moral values and to establish moral relativism as a new orthodoxy."[122] He elaborated:

> First, either through legislation but more frequently through judicial interpretation, secularists have been continually seeking to eliminate laws that reflect traditional moral norms.[123]

In short, progressives now vehemently denounce all those things that were once universally recognized as "good" and call them "no good." They find hateful the aspirations of the Founding Fathers to form a nation which "provides for limited government, while leaving 'the People' broadly at liberty to pursue our lives as individuals and through free

---

[121] Attorney General William P. Barr, Remarks to the Law School and the de Nicolas Center for Ethics and Culture at the University of Notre Dame, South Bend, IN, Oct. 11, 2019.

[122] *Id.*

[123] *Id.*

associations."[124] While this national founding proposition expresses the opposite of progressive desire to achieve an absolute transformation of society, progressives have an important ace up their sleeves. Progressives gleefully rely on a sad but correct predicament of mankind best encapsulated by Rebecca West. West lamented the fact that the majority of people are complacent, cannot learn complex truths, and forget even the basic simple truths associated with the pillars of establishment. They are perfect candidates for "victimhood." She wrote:

> The trouble with man is twofold – he cannot learn those truths that are too complex, and he forgets those truths that are too simple.[125]

Of course, Ms. West is not alone in this observation, many other thinkers have recognized and warned about it. For instance, in 1788 the State of Massachusetts proclaimed in their State Bill of Rights that "[a] frequent recurrence to fundamental principles is absolutely necessary to preserve the blessing of liberty and to maintain a free government."[126]

Before America even stood up as a Republic, early Western scholars such as John Locke, David Hume, Adam Smith, Baron de Montesquieu, and Jean-Jacques Rousseau wrote extensively on the subject, tying in as well their thoughts on civic humanism, natural rights, and the proper function of government in relation to the citizen. These scholars agreed with the premise that freedom loving people come together to form national entities so that the individual can, within the framework of a limited government, better protect and advance their God-given inherent rights to life, liberty, and property. They also recognized that for the establishment pillars to survive, their validity had to be

---

[124] *Id.*

[125] REBECCA WEST (CICELY ISABEL FAIRFIELD), THE MEANING OF TREASON 311 (1949).

[126] MASS. CONST. art. XVIII, https://law.justia.com/constitution/massachusetts/.

inculcated into the people. Edmond Burke said it best when he wrote: "All that is necessary for evil to prevail, is for good men to do nothing."[127]

Contrary to the status quo of the majority of countries of their day, men like Rousseau observed correctly that man "is born free" but "is everywhere in chains."[128] These men pointed out that government was formed to be the guardian of basic human freedoms, not the usurper. For instance, in his work entitled: SECOND TREATISE OF GOVERNMENT, John Locke wrote:

> The legislative or supreme authority cannot assume to itself a power to rule by extemporary, arbitrary decrees, but is bound to dispense justice, and to decide the rights of the subject by promulgated, standing laws, and known authorized judges.[129]

While the writings of these early scholars had a tremendous impact on America's Founding Fathers, it was their faith in an all-powerful Biblical God that gave them the strength and courage to face off against the finest military in the world—the British. Faced with the task of articulating a moral justification for their armed secession against the colonial rule of Great Britain, Thomas Jefferson and others were obliged to carefully translate their God-given inalienable natural rights into legal and enforceable rights. Apart from failing miserably to deal with the continued evil of human servitude practiced at that time by every colonial State (most assumed slavery would die a natural death within

---

[127] *See* Dan Cravens, *Evil Prevails When Good Men do Nothing*, Idaho State J. (Oct. 16, 2016), https://www.idahostatejournal.com/members/evil-prevails-when-good-men-do-nothing/article_1cf9a538-7a9a-5657-bb9f-25f728143821.html; *see also* Edmund Burke Quotes, Good Reads, https://www.goodreads.com/author/quotes/17142.Edmund_Burke.

[128] JEAN-JACQUES ROUSSEAU, THE SOCIAL CONTRACT (1762), https://www.earlymoderntexts.com/assets/pdfs/rousseau1762.pdf.

[129] JOHN LOCKE, SECOND TREATISE OF GOVERNMENT (1690), https://english.hku.hk/staff/kjohnson/PDF/LockeJohnSECONDTREAT ISE1690.pdf.

a few decades due to economic and moral pressures) the American drafters were brilliantly successful. In their Declaration of Independence to the British Crown, they declared that the individual, simply by virtue of his God-given being, possessed the "right to life, liberty, and the pursuit of happiness " The Declaration of Independence's powerful opening showed that the Founding Fathers were not inventing the ideals they embraced—they were embracing the Bible's establishment pillars. Undoubtedly these men were extremely courageous as all of them were signing their death warrant for treason if Britain won the war, but these new ideas were not new. The Founding Fathers were drawing on the wisdom of Biblical principles to bring together a proper balance between freedom and authority. Recognizing that freedom without authority is anarchy, and authority without freedom is tyranny, the Declaration of Independence proclaimed:

> We hold these truths to be self-evident, that all men are created equal, that they are endowed by their Creator with certain unalienable rights that among these are Life, Liberty, and the pursuit of Happiness. That to secure these rights, Governments are instituted among Men, deriving their just powers from the consent of the governed.[130]

In two sentences, the Framers laid out a fantastic manifesto that recognized the inherent right of men to exercise their God-given rights through a Republican government formed to protect the fundamental freedoms of its citizens. For the Americans, these rights were rooted in Divine providence which made them inalienable and morally justified *ab initio*.

With their freedom purchased through six long years of bloodshed on the battlefield, the colonial Americans produced one of the most phenomenal documents in the history of mankind—the Constitution of the United States of America. In point of fact, the United States of America was

---

[130] THE DECLARATION OF INDEPENDENCE para. 2 (U.S. 1776).

created as a representative democracy, i.e., a Republic; it is not a true direct democracy in the fashion of the ancient Greek city-state and is most assuredly not a socialist democracy.

Nations that toy with the concept of a direct democracy, where everyone votes regardless of contribution to society, court absolute disaster. In tracing the life expectancy of a democracy, it is interesting to note the words of historian Alexander Fraser Tytler (1748–1813), who wrote about the decline and fall of the Athenians. Tytler concluded:

> A democracy cannot exist as a permanent form of government. It can only exist until the voters discover that they can vote themselves money from the public treasury. From that moment on, the majority always votes for the candidates promising the most benefits from the public treasury with a result that a democracy always collapses over loose fiscal policy always followed by dictatorship.[131]

The Founding Fathers wisely restricted the franchise of participants and established three separate independent branches of government, with checks and balances, to ensure that the authority of the central government was truly limited, and the people truly represented. WEBSTER'S THIRD NEW INTERNATIONAL DICTIONARY defines a representative democracy as follows:

> A form of government in which the supreme power is vested in the people and exercised by them indirectly through a system of representation and delegated authority in which the people choose their officials and representatives at periodically held free elections. . . .[132]

---

[131] *See* Alexander Fraser Tytler, *Respectfully Quoted: A Dictionary of Quotations* (1989), https://www.bartleby.com/73/424.html.

[132] Democracy, MERRIAM-WEBSTER DICTIONARY, https://www.merriam-webster.com/dictionary/democracy.

Tragically, hidden in every form of virtuous government rest the seeds which will ultimately destroy it, for the ultimate matter of longevity is not really in the four establishment pillars themselves but in the character of the people who make up the nation. Virtue in the individual citizen is the critical ingredient. Richard Henry "Light Horse Harry" Lee III (the father of Robert E. Lee) once observed that when virtue is absent from the people, the nation cannot prosper. Lee wrote: "It is certainly true that a popular government cannot flourish without virtue in the people."[133]

In other words, the freedoms and blessings associated with the four establishment pillars cannot function without virtue. For example, when the employer possesses virtue there is no need for workers to form unions because the boss will take better care of the wants and needs of the employees than any union ever could. In contrast, an employer without virtue will operate the company with selfish interests without regard to honesty, integrity, or humanity. In turn, a worker with genuine virtue will work earnestly for his boss. Without virtue, a worker will produce little except slothfulness and deceit. Again, virtue can be defined as "doing a right thing in a right way."

Virtue cannot be legislated by the State. Before it can be reflected in the workings of society, this value must be taught in the home as a function of establishment pillar #3: the family. There is simply no question that all aspects of the four establishment pillars flourish when a nation is peopled with a majority of virtuous citizens.

Considering that the United States of America is just over 200 years old, Mr. Tytler went on to develop a fascinating general trend in the rise and fall of great nations. Collapse of great nations always comes from within and generally occurs because the people of that nation flunk what

---

[133] RICHARD HENRY LEE, MEMOIR OF THE LIFE OF RICHARD H. LEE, AND HIS CORRESPONDENCE WITH THE MOST DISTINGUISHED MEN IN AMERICA AND EUROPE (ed. 1825); *see also* Richard Henry Lee Quote, Lib Quotes, https://libquotes.com/richard-henry-lee/quote/lbv6k6l.

one might term the "prosperity test." Society reaches great levels of prosperity by adhering to the establishment pillars but then the people forget how they achieved such prosperity. The downward disorientation to reality reaches a "no return" point when people readily trade their virtue and freedom for a mess of pottage called socialism. They forgot the basic truths of establishment. Tytler wrote:

> The average age of the world's greatest civilizations has been 200 years. These nations have progressed through the following sequence:
>
> From bondage to spiritual faith;
>
> From spiritual faith to courage;
>
> From courage to liberty;
>
> From liberty to abundance;
>
> From abundance to selfishness;
>
> From selfishness to complacency;
>
> From complacency to apathy;
>
> From apathy to dependency;
>
> From dependency back to bondage.[134]

Of course, the Founders completely understood the viability of the establishment pillars and envisioned a nation described by Daniel Webster.

> A state of society characterized by tolerance toward minorities, freedom of expression, and respect for the essential dignity and worth of the human individual with equal opportunity for each to develop freely to his fullest capacity in a cooperative community.[135]

The factor that divides good government from evil government is in the degree to which the government allows

---

[134] *See* Alexander Fraser Tytler, *Alexander Fraser Tytler Quotes*, https://www.goodreads.com/quotes/108530-a-democracy-cannot-exist-as-a-permanent-form-of-government.

[135] DANIEL WEBSTER, WEBSTER'S THIRD NEW INTERNATIONAL DICTIONARY (1961).

the functioning of establishment pillars under the protection of the rule of law. Dictatorships have a pseudo "rule of law," but it is not based on principles of freedom. Accordingly, any so-called elections held in a totalitarian system can never be more than a cruel perversion of the concept. Clearly, a ruling system that provides its citizens with freedom of expression, peaceful assembly, a free market economy, and some degree of participation in government rests on establishment pillars. Thus, a monarchy, an aristocracy, or a representative democracy that rules for the common good of the citizen under the establishment pillar principles can each be positive manifestations of legitimacy. Other forms of government such as a tyranny or an oligarchy wield authority based solely on the self-interest of the ruling elite and refuse to embrace freedom.

In addressing the issue of writing democratic constitutions for the emerging democracies of Eastern Europe following the collapse of the Soviet Empire, Professor A. E. Dick Howard of the University of Virginia School of Law commented on this friction:

> The Bill of Rights of the United States Constitution declares what government may not do; it is what Justice Hugo Black once called a list of "thou shalt nots." The document reflects the view that the function of a bill of rights is to limit government's powers. Central and East European drafters have enlarged this meaning of "rights." A legacy of the twentieth-century notion of positive government, an age of entitlements, is bills of rights that declare affirmative rights. Such bills include, of course, the traditional negative rights, but they also spell out claims upon government, such as the right to an education, the right to a job, or the benefits of care in one's old age.[136]

---

[136] A.E. Dick Howard, *How Ideas Travel: Rights at Home and Abroad*, 22 Stetson L. Rev. 893 (1993), https://www.law.virginia.edu/system/files/faculty/hein/howard/22stetson_l_rev893_1993.pdf.

– You Cannot Use Freedom to Destroy Freedom –

The illusion of equality through social engineering by the force of a central government is the policy and propaganda of the socialist system. The true function of good government emphasizes freedom and self-determination which will always lead to varying degrees of social inequality. Faced with Lord Acton's often quoted truism that "power tends to corrupt, and absolute power corrupts absolutely,"[137] the government that adheres to principles of freedom and limited powers is much preferred. The progressive quest for affirmative third-generation rights for the people always leads to poverty and misery for both the people and the national entity.

But what if some of the people wanted to choose a political system that denies fundamental freedoms? Coming out of the Nazi era, the post-World War II German government was quick to address this question by enacting in their Basic Law a provision which holds that no citizen may use his freedom to destroy *freedom*. In other words, no political party that endorses non-democratic principles will be allowed to compete for office in an election, they will be banned. This is a core principle of the *streitbare Demokratie* (disputative democracy), which contains mechanisms to protect the system of values that it has established. The *Bundestag* (federal parliament), the *Bundesrat* (federal council), and the federal government are each entitled to file a motion to declare a political party as void. Accordingly, all Islamic political party movements that deny democratic principles under Sharia law would be banned. At Article 21:

> (1) Political parties shall participate in the formation of the political will of the people. They may be freely established. Their internal organization must conform to democratic principles. They must

---

[137] Letter from Lord Acton to Bishop Creighton (1887)(https://oll.libertyfund.org/quotes/214).

publicly account for their assets and for the source and use of their funds.

(2) Parties that, by reason of their aims or the behavior of their adherents, seek to undermine or abolish the free democratic basic order or to endanger the existence of the Federal Republic of Germany shall be unconstitutional. The Federal Constitutional Court shall rule on the question of unconstitutionality.

Indeed, once a true socialist party takes office, it will abolish all systems of freedom because it is the antithesis of freedom. This occurred recently in Venezuela when the socialists were voted into office and then immediately dismantled basic establishment pillars, causing great misery for the people and nation.[138] Another recent historical example of this strange paradox—where an extremist party manages to win at the ballot box—is found in the Algerian experience. When the first round of balloting in December 1991 went to the radical Taliban-styled Islamic Salvation Front (better known by its French acronym FIS), the Algerian military intervened to stop the extremists from taking power. Understanding that the FIS would not endorse principles of freedom if they took power, the Algerian Army banned the FIS and supported the secular State apparatus. Showing their true colors, the FIS then accelerated a murder and terror campaign (their tactic of choice was to slit the throat of anyone who did not agree with the Islamic movement) against the civilian population, resulting in the murder of nearly 200,000 people. Fortunately, the FIS's armed wing, the so-called Islamic Salvation Army,

---

[138] Venezuela, HUM. RTS. WATCH, https://www.hrw.org/world-report/2019/country-chapters/venezuela ("The government has been repressing dissent through often-violent crackdowns on street protests, jailing opponents, and prosecuting civilians in military courts."); *Venezuela's Nicolas Maduro: Dictator or defender of socialism?*, BBC News (Jan. 28, 2019), https://www.bbc.com/news/world-latin-america-20664349 (stating Maduro's accusations of undermining democracy and human rights violations since his election).

disbanded in January of 2000 and Algerians elected President Abdelaziz Bouteflika shortly thereafter. Although much remains to be done, President Boutelflika's Charter for Peace and National Reconciliation put the nation on the road to democratic reforms.

Chapter Four

The Pseudo-Pillars of Progressive Ideology

*"Let them alone; they are blind guides of the blind.
And if a blind man guides a blind man,
both will fall into a pit."*[139]

– Jesus of Nazareth

Encroachment on the establishment pillars is always for the so-called greater "good" of some group. For instance, in the early stages of the Communist Chinese revolution, the communists did away with narcotic dins and prostitution houses, winning the support of many of the local Christian churches for such impressive moralistic reforms. Then, when in power, the communists could not tolerate free thinkers and slaughtered the Chinese Christians wholesale.[140]

Hoisting the same flag of the greater good, American progressives seek a secular multicultural world (this is code for anything that denigrates Western civilization culture) which rejects the establishment pillars and replaces them

---

[139] Matt. 15:13.

[140] *See generally* Tatsuro Yamamoto & Sumiko Yamamoto, *The Anti-Christian Movement in China, 1922-1927,* 12 FAR EASTERN Q. 133 (1953) (providing a history of violence against Christians before the establishment of the Communist Party), *see also Valerie* Straus, *How Many Died? New Evidence Suggests Far Higher Numbers for the Victims of Mao Zedong's Era* (July 17, 1994), https://www.washingtonpost.com/archive/politics/1994/07/17/how-many-died-new-evidence-suggests-far-higher-numbers-for-the-victims-of-mao-zedongs-era/01044df5-03dd-49f4-a453-a033c5287bce/ (suggesting the numbers of Christians killed was much higher than originally thought).

with progressive ones. Fueled by the hot fires of political correctness, progressive thinking is insidious in its utter hypocrisy. Claiming to embrace tolerance, the truth is that progressives are only tolerant of those that agree with them. All others are targeted for great smears on their name. Indeed, when free speech is based on consensus, there is no free speech!

The purity test that all must swear allegiance to views the present and the past through the fantasy looking glass of "presentism." Presentism is a radical leftist vetting process which "mercilessly subjects history and historical figures to a contemporary social enlightenment"[141] standard. Talibanesque in outcome, it cares nothing for context, common sense, or truth. To be certain, presentism is not just an attack on history and the validity of the establishment pillars, it seeks to rewrite the former and supplant the later.

In a nutshell, all progressive thinking is evil. As with the Genesis tree of the knowledge of "good and evil," progressivism is easily defined as being the exact opposite of the thinking of God, to include His intrinsic establishment pillars. But to fully realize how the onslaught of progressive thinking operates to supplant the establishment pillars, one needs to understand that it has its own false or pseudo-pillars. These substitute pillars are three in number: (1) equality; (2) brotherhood; and (3) social justice.

– Equality –

While the Don Quixote quest for "equality" is nothing new, what is disturbing is the fact that millions upon millions of Sanchos blindly follow the madness with barely a hint of dissent. In fact, the fallen angel Lucifer used this very same tactic to deceive Eve in perfect environment with an absurdly arrogant offer of equality with God. She was deceived by the lie and chose it resulting in her immediate

---

[141] Ross. K. Baker, *Voices: Democrats Foolishly Purge Heroes*, USA TODAY, August 11, 2015, at A2.

spiritual death—separation from perfect God.[142] Adam also followed suit in his own volitional choice and he was not deceived when he did it! Genesis 6:6-7 states:

> The Lord God commanded the man, saying, "From any tree of the garden you may eat freely; but from the tree of the knowledge of good [*tob*] and evil you shall not eat [*akal* – disobeying God is a sin], for in the day [*yom*] that you eat from it you will surely [*muth* (die)—spiritual death] die [*muth* (die)—physical death]."[143]

Literally the warning from God was: "dying *spiritually* you will die *physically* at a future date." In other words, their spiritual death—separation from fellowship with perfect God—was immediate, but their physical death took some time.

Then, once in this state of spiritual death, it is fascinating to note that their first act together was to make fig leaves into a covering for their nakedness. Obviously, both bodies were fantastically beautiful in form and feature and they had frolicked about in their birthday suits for an unknown amount of time—perhaps thousands of years. Why the sudden interest in clothes? It was not the weather or the elements.

The Bible makes the answer clear, the clothes making was the first act of human equality. In essence they were both infected with the virus of evil in their new natures and had to find a solution to their dilemma of separation from God. In quick step, they sought the human good of equality under the lie that "if we are right with each other"—they covered up their obvious physical differences to look more equal in appearance—"then we will be right with God." In great arrogance, they were asking God to accept their human good works of equality so that they would once again be in a fellowship relationship and acceptable to God. However,

---

[142] Gen. 3:1-2; Deut. 30:19.

[143] Gen. 2:6-7.

when perfect God approached them in the cool of the evening they immediately hid from His presence, as human good and spiritual death cannot stand in the presence of perfect God.[144] Genesis 3:7-10 tells the story.

> Then the eyes of both of them [Adam and the woman after they sinned] were opened, and they knew [*yada* (to learn to know)] that they were naked; and they sewed fig leaves together and made themselves loin coverings [they engaged in acts of human good to make themselves equal]. They heard the sound of the Lord God walking in the garden in the cool of the day, and the man and his wife hid themselves from the presence of the Lord God among the trees of the garden [human good in a state of sin cannot stand in the presence of perfect Divine good]. Then the Lord God called to the man [Adam], and said to him, "Where are you [*ay* (why arc you where you are)]?" He said, "I heard the sound of You in the garden, and I was afraid because I was naked; so I hid [*chaba* (secretly conceal)] myself."[145]

In fact, the concept of equality is a very pliable construct, depending on what one seeks to accomplish. In the first instance of its use which was targeted towards humans, it was employed by Satan to deceive Eve to rebel against God and in the second use, Adam and Eve employed it in an attempt to gain the approbation of God. Although most progressives today flatly reject the notion of a Biblical God, if they even care to think about the nature and person of God at all, they nevertheless desperately cling to the equality factor as the end all and be all of human existence and the

---

[144] After Adam and Eve believed the gospel of salvation about the promised coming "seed of the woman" who would die for their sins, per Genesis 3:15, God took off the fig leaves and clothed them with the skin of an animal, which represented the future Messiah's work on the Roman cross in circa A.D. 30. From then on the sacrifice of the innocent animal was a teaching tool related salvation.

[145] Gen. 3:7-10.

meaning of life. On the one hand it justifies them in promoting various social agendas which they esteem as "good" and on the other hand, it makes them feel accepted and self-important. Of course, their view is not God's view. Jesus pointed this out to the religious leaders of His day on many occasions, as in Luke 16:15.

> And He [Jesus] said to them [the religious leaders], "You are those who justify themselves in the sight of men, but God knows your hearts; for that which is highly esteemed among men [the equality factor of human good] is detestable [*delugma* (a foul thing)] in the sight of God."[146]

Interestingly, as with the illogical battle cry of the terrorist rabble during the French Revolution—"liberty, equality, fraternity (brotherhood)"—equality and liberty cannot coexist. As a rallying slogan it may sound attractive, but "liberty and equality" are polar opposites. A truly free person that is allowed to exercise his liberty to make various choices in life will soon be "unequal" with his fellow man. In fact, true liberty operating in society demands inequality as its logical outcome.

– Brotherhood –

Progressive ideology also promotes a "brotherhood" relationship for all mankind, or rather all those that think like they think. Proponents falsely assert that since all humans are "brothers"—the so-called brotherhood of man—then they should share resources as one big happy commune. Regardless of the fact that those not considered to be "in line" with the brotherhood are subject to relentless assaults on their name and reputation, this wonderful condition of leftist brotherhood is allegedly based on a glorious personal "love" for all people. This is a second key element of deception in progressivism and it is undeniably a crafty argument to make. I mean, who is against "loving" their

---

[146] Lk. 16:15.

fellow man? The answer, of course, is that discerning readers of the Bible are against such nonsense.

The brotherhood of all concept is not the Bible's view. For one thing, the Bible most certainly teaches that God is not the father of all mankind and that believers in Christ are not "brothers" with all those who choose to reject Christ's free offer of salvation by grace. In fact, the Bible relates that Lucifer the Devil is the father of many humans on this planet. Quite frankly, for example, anyone who rejects Christ for salvation is termed a *nothos* (bastard) in Hebrews 12:8. Furthermore, in Romans 5:10, Colossians 1:21, and Ephesians 2:11-15 the unbeliever is also called the enemy of God. In John 8:44-45 Jesus made it very clear that there is no fatherhood of God and no brotherhood of man.

> You [Jesus was speaking to the religious leaders of His day] are of *your* father [*pater*] the devil [*diabolos* (slanderer) – Satan], and you want to do the desires of your father. He was a murderer from the beginning and does not stand in the truth [*aletheia* (what is true in any matter under consideration)] because there is no truth in him. Whenever he speaks a lie, he speaks from his own *nature*, for he is a liar [*pseustes*] and the father of lies. But because I [Jesus] speak the truth, you do not believe Me.[147]

– Love

In turn, armchair students of the Bible who assert that Christians are commanded to "love" everyone are absolutely misguided and know nothing of the original Greek text. The exegetical problem with the so-called love everyone crowd rests in their absolute misunderstanding of the type of "love" that is commanded in the Bible. Their gross misinterpretation of the Bible in this regard is deeply disconcerting.

---

[147] Jn. 8:44-45.

Christians and those that understand the establishment pillars know that the command to love their fellow man is not associated with the concept of personal love at all, but rather it is an impersonal love attitude towards all mankind that is commanded. The bottom line is that while Christians are commanded to maintain a relaxed mental attitude of love for all mankind, it is never a personal love for fellow humans that God commands, but rather an impersonal love for fellow humans. Although the difference between personal and impersonal love is quite distinct and clearly presented in the Bible, very few people seem to understand the distinction. The difference, of course, is fantastic and those few that comprehend this fact are greatly relieved once it becomes evident. As such, it is well worth taking the ink to describe it herein.

The proper understanding of the command to love your fellow man demands a brief study on the topic. As with the English language, the word love in the original Greek of the New Testament is used to describe a variety of concepts and the context will determine the meaning. There are two main words translated from the Greek as "love" in the New Testament—*agape* and *philos*. As in the English, the words are used to describe one or more of the following four categories of love:

(a) Category I: towards God as the object. This is a *personal* love directly related to the attractiveness of the object, God.[148]

(b) Category II: towards a member of the opposite sex in marriage as the object. This is a *personal* love directly related to the attractiveness of the object, the spouse.[149]

---

[148] *See, e.g.,* Deut. 6:5; Rom. 8:35; 1 Jn. 4:19.

[149] *See, e.g.,* S. S. 8:6-7.

(c) Category III: towards close friends as the object. This is a *personal* love related to the attractiveness of the object, the friend.[150]

(d) Category IV: towards all members of the human race as the object. This is an *impersonal* love not related to the object whatsoever, other humans.[151]

You will immediately note that Category IV impersonal love is absolutely different from the other three as it is not dependent on the attractiveness of the object at all. The noun *agape* and verb *agapao* are always used to describe this technical theological concept which, when properly used, is the preeminent problem solving device for Christians in their interaction with other members of the human race—both fellow Christians and all others.[152] In short, *agape* impersonal love when employed in its technical meaning

---

[150] *See, e.g.,* Jn. 15:13; 1 Sam. 18:1; 2 Sam. 1:26. Jesus in His humanity expressed a personal love for his friend Lazarus in Jn. 11:33-37.

> When Jesus therefore saw her [Mary] weeping [*klaio* (to mourn; to weep)], and the Jews who came with her *also* weeping, He was deeply moved in spirit [*pneuma*] and was troubled [*tarasso* (to agitate)], and said, "Where have you laid him [Lazarus]?" They said to Him, "Lord, come and see." Jesus wept [*dakruo* (to shed tears)]. So, the Jews were saying, "See how He loved [*phileo* (personal love)] him!" But some of them said, "Could not this man, who opened the eyes of the blind man, have kept this man also from dying [*apothnesko*]?"

[151] *See, e.g.,* Jn. 3:16 (employed by God in salvation).

> For God so loved [*agapao* – impersonal love] the world [*kosmos*], that He gave His only begotten [*monogenes* (single of its kind; uniquely born)] Son [Jesus Christ], that whoever believes [*pisteuo* – faith in Christ for salvation] in Him shall not perish [*apollumi* (to put out of the way entirely; to utterly destroy)], but have eternal [*aonios* (without beginning and end)] life [*zoe*].

[152] *See, e.g.,* 1 Cor. 13:1.3

> But now faith [*pistis* – relying on a promise of God], hope [*elpis* (confident expectation)], love [*agape* – impersonal love], abide [*meno* (remain)] these three [they are problem solving devices]; but the greatest [*megas*] of these is love [*agape* – impersonal love is the greatest of the three to deal with problems in life].

places all the focus and attention on the integrity of the subject, not the attractiveness or unattractiveness of the object. When *agape* impersonal love is applied to a particular episode of life, everything is dependent on the subject's character not the object's character. Accordingly, the object can be hateful, deceitful, vindictive, jealous, or spiteful to the subject and yet the subject does not react with any type of sin—they maintain a relaxed mental attitude toward the object.

As illustrated by the chart below, *agape* impersonal love draws its power by concentrating on the integrity inherent in the subject, not the attractiveness of the object.

> **I** [the subject] love [transitive verb, *agapao*] **you** [the object].

Technical Use of *Agape* Impersonal Love

With the employment of *agape* impersonal love, the Christian cannot get upset, frustrated, jealous, disappointed, etc. For example, if the object lies about the Christian, the Christian employs impersonal *agape* love and doesn't respond in kind. 1 Corinthians 13:4-7 describes in detail the characteristics of impersonal love and even the novice can understand that it is not a personal love that is in focus here.

> Love [*agape* – impersonal love] is patient [*makrothumeo* (to persevere bravely under unjust treatment)], love [*agape* – impersonal love] is kind [*chresteuomai* (to show one's self mild)] and is not jealous [*zeloo*]; love [*agape* – impersonal love] does not brag [*perpereuomai* (to boast one's self)] and is not arrogant [*phusioo* (to cause to swell up)], does not act unbecomingly [*aschemoneo* (has good manners, not rude)]; it does not seek [*zeteo*] its own [not preoccupied with self], is not provoked

97

[*paroxumo* (to arouse to anger)], does not take into account a wrong suffered, does not rejoice in unrighteousness [*adikia* (injustice)], but rejoices with the truth [*aletheia* (what is true in any matter under consideration)]; bears [*stego* (to keep secret the errors or faults of others)] all things, believes [*pisteuo* (to think to be true)] all things, hopes [*elpizo*] all things, endures [*hupomeno* (to persevere under misfortunes and trials)] all things.[153]

Again, it is absolutely true that Believers are commanded to have *agape* impersonal love for all mankind, never a personal love. There are many verses associated with this command to include 1 John 3:23.

This is His [God the Father] commandment [*entole* (an order)], that we believe [*pisteuo*] in the name of His Son Jesus Christ, and love [*agape* – impersonal love] one another, just as He [Jesus] commanded us.[154]

Indeed, Christians are commanded to maintain an *agape* impersonal love even for their enemies.[155] If the object hates, the believer does not hate back—he employs the idiom of "turning the other cheek." Note, however, that "turn the other cheek" is an idiom only—it does not apply to an actual physical attack. The Christian is absolutely authorized to employ physical self-defense to protect himself, his family, or his nation which he can do while maintaining a relaxed mental attitude of *agape* impersonal love. In Matthew 5:38-39, Jesus used the idiom to describe impersonal love:

---

[153] 1 Cor. 13:4-7.

[154] *See also*, Gal. 5:14; Mk. 12:31; 1 Jn. 3:23; 4:7, 11, 20-21; Lk. 10:27; Matt. 5:38-39; 22:39; Jn. 15:12, 17; Js. 2:8; Lev. 19:18; Rom. 13:9.

[155] *See, e.g.,* Matt. 5:43-47; Luke 6:27, 35. Matt. 5:44:

But I [Jesus] say to you [His disciples], love [*agapao* – impersonal love] your enemies [*echthros* (a man that is hostile)] and pray for those who persecute [*dioko*] you.

You have heard that it was said [the Mosaic Law], "An eye for an eye, and a tooth for a tooth." But I [Jesus Christ] say to you, do not resist [*anthistemi* (to set one's self against)] an evil [*poneros*] person; but whoever slaps you on your right cheek, turn the other to him also [idiom for *agape* impersonal love].[156]

In turn, God can only have an impersonal love towards those who do not accept salvation by grace—there is no attractiveness in the object.[157] Since God can only express *agape* impersonal love for unbelieving mankind, His subsequent work to provide salvation was not based on the attractiveness of humans (the object), but on His own perfect character/integrity (the subject).[158] On the other hand, God's

---

[156] Matt. 5:38-39.

[157] *See, e.g.,* Rom. 5:8-10.

But God demonstrates [*sunistao* (to put together by way of composition; to show; to prove)] His own love [*agape* – impersonal love] toward us, in that while we were yet sinners [*hamartolos* – the unbeliever under spiritual death], Christ died [*apothnesko* (of violent death; of eternal death; to be subject to eternal misery in hell)] for us. Much more [*polus mallon* (much more; it stands to greater reason)] then, having now been justified [*dikaioo* (to render righteous) – the believer has the Righteousness of God imputed to him at the second of belief and is now rendered righteous and acceptable to Perfect God] by His blood [*aima* – the work of Christ on the cross to bear all sin], we shall be saved [*sozo* (to deliver) – delivered into the Kingdom of Heaven at the second of belief] from the wrath [*orge*] *of God* through [*dia* (by means of)] Him [Jesus Christ]. For if while we were enemies [*echthros* – as unbelievers prior to salvation] we were reconciled [*katallasso* (to receive one into favor)] to God through [*dia* (by means of)] the death [*thanatos* (death with the implied idea of future misery in hell)] of His Son, much more, having been reconciled [*katallasso* – the Believer receives God's Righteousness], we shall be saved [*sozo* (to deliver) – to deliver to the status of a resurrection body] by His life.

[158] *See, e.g.,* 1 Jn. 4:9-10.

By this the love [*agape* – impersonal love] of God was manifested [*phaneroo*] in us [Believers], that God has sent His only begotten [*monogenes* (single of its kind)] Son [Jesus

personal love is activated towards a human when that person believes in Christ and receives God's own Righteousness imputed to his soul/human spirit in a split second of time.[159] Because the believer possesses God's Righteousness, God now has a maximum personal love for him and the believer is now a child of God.

Personal love is commonly designated by use of the noun *philos* (to have personal attachment as a matter of sentiment or feeling; affection for; personal love) or the verb *phileo*. Personal *philos* love places the emphasis on the attractiveness of the object.[160]

> **I** [the subject] love [transitive verb, *phileo*]
> **YOU** [the object].

Personal Love

Personal love is where the entire emphasis is placed on the object. Again, the Biblical command is for *agape* impersonal love towards all mankind, never personal love. The emphasis of impersonal love is on the integrity of the subject, not the nature of the object. As stated, with impersonal love rooted in his soul, the Christian can "turn

---

Christ] into the world so that we might live [*zao* (to have true life)] through Him. In this is love [*agape* – impersonal love], not that we loved [*agapao* (to love dearly)] God, but that He loved [*agapao* – impersonal love] us and sent His Son *to be* the propitiation [*hilasmos* (an appeasing)] for our sins [*hamartia*].

[159] *See, e.g.,* Jn. 16:27.

For the Father Himself loves [*phileo* (personal love)] you [the Believer], because you have loved [*phileo* (personal love)] Me [Jesus Christ] and have believed that I came forth from the Father.

[160] *See* RICHARD TRENCH, SYNONYMS OF THE NEW TESTAMENT 41 (2000), (states that *philos* is the "stronger" word for love in the Greek than the general usages of the word *agape* (to love dearly).

the other cheek" which means he is able to exercise tolerance of others and resist the temptation to respond with hatred or vituperation when subjected to insults. In direct contrast, personal love places all the emphasis on the object—some characteristic possessed by the object of your personal love is extremely attractive and might for humans include physical attraction or intellectual attraction.

Accordingly, you can't have personal love for something that you don't know. Thus, only a Christian that knows a maximum amount of Bible doctrine in the status quo of a mature believer can love God with a *philos* personal love. In turn, with a personal love for God by increased knowledge the mature believer is better able to love all mankind with *agape* impersonal love. While God loves all Believers equally with a personal love—because all Believers possess His Righteousness—most Believers do not have a personal love for God. This fact is set out in 1 Peter 1:6-8 and Romans 8:28-30.[161]

---

[161] Rom. 8:28-30:

And we [Paul and all mature believers] know [*heneka* (on account of)] that God causes all things to work together [*sunergeo*] for good [*agathos* (good of intrinsic value) – Divine good] to those who love [*agapao* (to love dearly)] God [only the Believer who reaches maturity with a maximum amount of knowledge about God can love God], to those who are called [*kletos* (called; invited to a banquet)] according [*kata* (according to a norm or standard)] to *His* purpose [*prosthesis* (a predetermined plan)]. For those whom He foreknew [*proginosko* (to have knowledge beforehand) – the humans that would believe in Christ], He also predestined [*proorizo* (to decide beforehand) – God made provisions to get the positive volition Christian to the status of maturity] *to become* conformed [*summorphos* (having the same form as another)] to the image of His Son, so that He would be the firstborn [the resurrection] among many brethren [*adelphos* (brothers)]; and these whom He predestined [*proorizo*], He also called [*kaleo* (to call aloud; to invite)]; and these whom He called, He also justified [*dikaioo* (to render righteous) – by receiving God's Righteousness]; and these whom He justified, He also glorified [*doxazo* (to honor) – by the giving of rewards].

In summary, while Christians are commanded in the Bible to have personal *philos* for love for God (note: *agape* is also used in a non-technical sense to mean "personal love" in some verses), they are only commanded to have an impersonal love for all mankind.[162]

The bottom line is clear. When progressives talk about brotherhood and love they deceive. Mankind has seen this lie played out on many stages in the past. Be it the emotionally charged brotherhood frenzy of the French Revolution, or the sweetness and light "comrade" labels of communist Russia and China, all such movements quickly settle on great violence, suffering, and death in the name of "promoting brotherhood." The horrible irony is written in volumes of human blood.

– Social Justice –

The third progressive building block is "social justice." Closely set next to the false flag of equality, this pillar holds that a society based upon the establishment pillars is "unjust" and until an all-powerful central government can provide for true equality in society, it is the solemn duty of every individual to organize into groups in order to perform any number of things for the "downtrodden." This even includes the criminal elements in society. After all, they claim, criminals only commit crimes due to the unjust environment created by the operation of the establishment pillars which are devoid of social justice. In particular, social justice warriors readily reject establishment pillars #1 (individualism), #3 (nuclear family) and #4 (nationalism/patriotism). All of them seem oblivious to the obvious and rational bottom line conclusion of the matter regarding the existence of crime in society—criminals cause crime.

In his ground-breaking book on criminal behavior, entitled INSIDE THE CRIMINAL MIND, Dr. Stanton E.

---

[162] *See, e.g.,* 2 Cor. 5:14; 1 Cor. 16:22; Rom. 5:5; 8:28; 1 Pet. 1:8.

Samenow, Jr., summed it all up quite succinctly: criminals cause crime.

> Criminals cause crime—not bad neighborhoods, inadequate parents, television, schools, drugs, or unemployment. Crime resides in the minds of human beings and is not caused by social conditions. Once we as a society recognize this simple fact, we shall take measures radically different from current ones. To be sure, we shall continue to remedy intolerable social conditions for this is worthwhile in and of itself. But we shall not expect criminals to change because of such efforts.[163]

In short, social justice places all the emphasis on human efforts to "reform" society's establishment pillars and thereby make the world a "better place."[164] Of course, the

---

[163] STANTON E. SAMENOW, JR., INSIDE THE CRIMINAL MIND 6 (1984).

[164] LEWIS SPERRY CHAFER, SYSTEMATIC THEOLOGY, Vol. 1&2 110-111 (1976).

> Great religious activities are possible without coming into complication with saving faith. It is possible to fight against sin and not present the Savior, or to urge the highest Scriptural ideals and yet offer no reasonable way of attainment. There is a strange fascination about these undertakings which are humanitarian, and are religious only in form and title. And there is a strange attractiveness in the leader who announces that he is not concerned with the doctrines of the Bible, because the helping of humanity is his one passion and care. . . . Who can be the god of these systems? * * * Certain religious systems which are in no way related to the Bible and have continued for millenniums—including the ancient pagan systems and spiritism—have held the devotion of uncounted millions and bear every evidence of being inspired by Satan. The moral problem, which is felt to some degree by every human being, is seized upon by almost every unscriptural system. The idea that man will stand on a basis of personal worthiness has been the chief heresy, opposing the central doctrine of grace, from the time of Christ's death to the present hour. It so permeates the church that few who preach are able to exclude it from their attempts at gospel preaching. It is safe to say that wherever the element of human merit is allowed to intrude into the presentation of the plan of salvation, the message is satanic to

Biblical view is that Satan is the ruler of the world and that the world can only be "improved" to the extent of individual or collective efforts to abide by the mandates of the establishment pillars. Thus, while evil will never be eradicated by humans, it can be better addressed. At most, the social justice warrior can only whitewash the Devil's world—he cannot change it.

The primary Bible passage used by some progressives to promote the false doctrine of social justice as a means to gain the approbation of God and man is found in Matthew 25:34-46. Although these verses have absolutely nothing to do with salvation or the efficacy of the establishment pillars, they are nonetheless championed by the "human good works and social justice crowd" as the central means to curry favor and acceptance with God and man by engaging in do-good efforts for other humans to include feeding (free), housing (free), clothing (free), or visiting them in prison.

First, this absolutely false interpretation of Matthew 25:34-46 contradicts the hundreds upon hundreds of verses in the Bible which irrevocably teach salvation by means of non-meritorious grace totally apart from any human deeds whatsoever. Nowhere does Biblical Christianity teach that one must perform acts of human charity to be saved or rack up "brownie points" with God. Chapters 24 and 25 of Matthew deals exclusively with eschatology. Jesus is speaking about a future seven-year time called in dispensational theology the Tribulation which is then immediately followed by His physical Second Coming to the earth at the Mount of Olives outside of Jerusalem. In that context, Matthew 24:34-46 refers specifically to those Tribulational Gentile believers of that future time who risk their lives to house, clothe, feed, and give comfort to certain Jewish evangelists around the globe that were being hunted down and killed by the forces and agents of Satan per

---

that extent. The ministers of Satan proclaim personal righteousness as the ground of the individual's right relations to God (2 Corinthians 11:13-15).

Revelation 7:4-17 and 14:1-20. Matt. 25:34-46 simply states that these future humans, who are already saved believers, will receive special rewards in the eternal state for their actions in this context.

– Hating Americanism –

Progressives abhor Americanism and reject the exceptionalism it implies. What does Americanism mean? What things must you believe in for you to support the concept of Americanism? Because progressives correctly associate the word Americanism with all those who support the establishment pillars, the word is detestable to them. And they are right. Americans who believe in Americanism recognize the establishment pillars as truth and strongly support them. Americans who do not are kidding themselves and simply selfishly enjoying the prosperity produced by their betters—those who believe in Americanism.

Social problems in society can never be solved by legislation washed in equality, brotherhood, or social justice. In fact, social engineering to alter the establishment pillars always causes greater problems. While all citizens should be charitable in their individual capacity and the government does have a limited obligation to establish certain safety nets to "promote the general welfare," viable actions to better address social problems must be accomplished by or via a very strong adherence to the pillars of establishment.

The false propaganda from the "peaceful" progressive is that as long as one sincerely tries his best to seek equality, work for social justice, make the world a better place, and love his fellow man, he will obtain great happiness. The "aggressive" progressive is not content to tolerate opposing views and actively targets the establishment pillars using, if necessary, overt violence to achieve their ends. Both categories hate the truth.

America can only ride the crests of the waves of history so long as it follows the dictates of the establishment pillars.

This great nation will most surely drown in a sea of hypocrisy if it trades its freedom for a mess of "equality, love, and social justice" pottage. The real genius of the United States is that this nation of immigrants has managed to unite all the disparate parts by recognizing the validity of the establishment principles. We call this Americanism. While the establishment pillars were not designed to address the problem of eternal salvation—the grace provision of Biblical Christianity asserts salvation is by faith alone in the work of Jesus Christ alone—they will provide a wonderful life on this earth that is filled with great stability, prosperity, and satisfaction.

Chapter Five

The Trump Judges

"This was an Obama judge."[165]

– Donald J. Trump

The methodology for selecting federal judges is rather straightforward. The Constitution provides that the President shall select qualified candidates and that the Senate shall confirm them.[166] Given that a particular president is most certainly going to appoint men and women to the bench that reflect his ideological/political positions, the confirmation process not only allows for a period of questioning and deliberation, but much political maneuvering generally occurs before a final up or down vote is taken by the full Senate. Up until recently, Senate rules and custom mandated that federal judges were approved by a super majority of the Senate, sixty votes, but now, based on a rule change imposed by Obama era Democrats when they controlled the Senate, only a simple majority vote is required.[167]

In terms of picking Supreme Court nominees, President Trump early on in his run for office vowed to appoint conservative originalists, even announcing a pool of potential candidates from a list provided by the Federalist

---

[165] *See* Adam Liptak, *Chief Justice Defends Judicial Independence After Trump Attacks 'Obama Judge'*, N.Y. TIMES (Nov. 21, 2018), https://www.nytimes.com/2018/11/21/us/politics/trump-chief-justice-roberts-rebuke.html.

[166] U.S. CONST. art. II, § 2, cl. 2.

[167] *See* Russell Berman, *How Democrats Paved the Way for the Confirmation of Trump's Cabinet*, ATLANTIC (Jan. 20, 2017), https://www.theatlantic.com/politics/archive/2017/01/democrats-trump-cabinet-senate/513782/.

Society.[168]   Although President Trump later added some names to that list, these new individuals were also firmly in the camp of the originalist.   Within his first two years President Trump picked lower federal court judges Neil Gorsuch and Bret Kavanaugh to sit on the Supreme Court. Gorsuch was a replacement for deceased Antonin Scalia and Kavanaugh would fill the slot vacated by a retiring Anthony Kennedy.   While Gorsuch simply replaced a slot filled by another originalist, Kavanaugh, an originalist, replaced someone who was not.   Thus, the seating of Associate Justice Kavanaugh was a severe blow to the living constitutionalist crowd.   Both men were confirmed and sworn in, although neither received a super majority vote from the then Republican held Senate.[169]

In addition to filling two slots on the Supreme Court, the Republican controlled Senate reached an historic milestone in September 2019, by voting on and installing in office 150 Article III judges,[170] with 43 circuit court judges.[171]   By January 1, 2020, the number had swelled to 187. Considering that there are a total of 870 authorized federal judgeships—nine on the Supreme Court, 179 on the federal courts of appeals, nine on the court of international trade, and 674 district federal courts—the number of Trump fills is

[168] *See* Lydia Wheeler, *Meet the Powerful Group Behind Trump's Judicial Nominations*, HILL (Nov. 16, 2017, 6:00 AM), https://thehill.com/regulation/court-battles/360598-meet-the-powerful-group-behind-trumps-judicial-nominations.

[169] *See* Alana Abramson, *Brett Kavanaugh Confirmed to Supreme Court After Fight That Divided America*, TIME (Oct. 7, 2018, 5:11 PM), http://time.com/5417538/bett-kavanaugh-confirmed-senate-supreme-court/.

170 *See* Kevin Schaul and Kevin Uhrmacher, *How Trump is Shifting the Most Important Courts in the Country,* WASH. POST (Sep. 4, 2018), https://www.washingtonpost.com/graphics/2018/politics/trump-federal-judges/?utm_term=.c6c76f4031ab.

[171] *See* Alex Swoyer, *"Historic Milestone," Senate Confirms 150th Trump Judicial Nominee*, WASH. TIMES (Sept. 11, 2019) https://www.washingtontimes.com/news/2019/sep/11/senate-confirms-150th-trump-judicial-nominee/.

impressive. Of particular note is the impact that Trump has had on the Ninth Circuit Court of Appeals, which conservatives have often railed against due to its extreme liberal leanings. Under President Trump, a dramatic change has occurred with 10 of its active 29 sitting judges now Trump appointees. The Trump record of accomplishment is impressive and far exceeds the Obama effort during this same period of time (74 federal district court judges and 20 circuit court judges).

With well over a hundred more vacancies to fill in the immediate future, much of the credit for the "fast track" movement goes to the Senate Republican majority leader, Mitch McConnell. For example, to further speed up the process of Trump federal judge confirmations, McConnell has reduced the amount of Senate debate for the lower-level federal judicial nominees from 30 hours to only 2. The Senate minority leader Chuck Schumer is helpless to stop the Trump steamroll and with a second term in office and a Republican controlled Senate, Trump will only continue to rack up more and more originalist jurists.

– Oh, Really Now? –

In late November 2018, President Trump publicly complained about an Obama appointed federal judge who ordered the Trump Administration to resume accepting asylum seekers who entered the United States illegally from Mexico.[172] Trump called the California district judge, Joe S. Tigar, an "Obama judge" and went on to lambast the liberal Ninth Circuit as a "disgrace."[173] The next day, Chief Justice John Roberts publicly responded to President Trump in an attempt to defend what he deemed to be an unwarranted attack on "judicial independence." Although Roberts did not specifically deny that judges might not be ideologically

---

[172] *Id.*

[173] *Id.*

detached from the particular president who recommended them for office, he nevertheless blistered at the label:

> We do not have Obama judges or Trump judges, Bush judges or Clinton judges. What we have is an extraordinary group of dedicated judges doing their level best to do equal right to those appearing before them. That independent judiciary is something we should all be thankful for.[174]

While it is undeniable that the judiciary must remain independent of the other two branches of government, Justice Roberts certainly knows that we do in fact have "Obama judges" and "Trump judges." The expression "Obama judge" used by Trump does not imply that judges do the bidding of the president that appointed them, but it does recognize the reality that such judges were chosen precisely because they embraced, to some degree, the same ideological stance of the person that choose them. The result? An Obama judge or a Trump judge, as the case may be.

As previously covered, judges do not interpret the U.S. Constitution and the laws of the United States in the same way. An Obama judge will generally fall into the category of the living constitutionalist while the Trump judge will generally fall into the camp of the originalist. Understanding the obvious implications of all this, plaintiffs will file lawsuits in federal district courts that they calculate will rule in their favor. This certainly was the case in those lower court challenges to President Trump's Travel ban, which the Supreme Court ultimately upheld in *Trump v. Hawaii*[175]— plaintiffs specially sought out living constitutionalist judges. All sides do this. In fact, they would be grossly irresponsible if they didn't. According to one source:

---

[174] *See* Adam Liptak, *Chief Justice Defends Judicial Independence After Trump Attacks 'Obama Judge'*, N.Y. TIMES (Nov. 21, 2018), https://www.nytimes.com/2018/11/21/us/politics/trump-chief-justice-roberts-rebuke.html.

[175] Trump v. Hawaii, 138 S. Ct. 2392 (2018).

Plaintiffs challenging the Obama administration's health care, immigration and other programs often filed their lawsuits in Texas before conservative judges. The State of Texas alone sued the Obama administration at least 48 times, according to a survey conducted by *The Texas Tribune*.[176]

Whatever else is said about the contentious 2018 Kavanaugh Senate hearings, it is certain that both sides of the ideological divide realized the importance of selecting new federal judges, with Supreme Court appointees being the crown jewels. Progressives certainly understand it, as almost every one of their agenda items to remake America in their image have resulted not from the work of the elected legislative branch of government, but by progressive living constitutionalist judges.

Indeed, when the Republican controlled Senate appointed its 150th federal district judge in September 2019, Marge Baker, the executive vice president of the far-left group People for the American Way engaged in the usual emotional name calling to express her frustration regarding conservative judges that would not advance the progressive social agenda of the left.[177] Baker said:

> As of today's confirmation votes, Trump and McConnell [Speaker of the Senate] have confirmed 150 judges to the federal bench—a group that can overwhelmingly be described as narrow-minded and elitist, favoring corporations and the powerful over the interests of all Americans.[178]

In this regard, President Trump and his Republican majority Senate[179] have done a yeoman's job in appointing

---

[176] *See* Liptak, *supra* note 184.

[177] Swoyer, *supra* note 181.

[178] *Id.*

[179] The 2018 mid-term elections saw the Republican majority grow from 51 to 53 in the U.S. Senate. *See* Mary Kay Linge, *Why Republicans Actually Have the Upper Hand After the Midterms*, N.Y. POST (Nov. 10,

federal judges. In addition, as long as the Republican Party has a majority in the Senate, President Trump will have the upper hand, showing no desire for selecting a compromise candidate that sits somewhere in the ideological center. Speculation aside, the number of Trump judges will most certainly grow with perhaps the addition of another Supreme Court originalist.[180]

For those that are opposed to the appointment of more originalists to the Court, there is always a glimmer of hope. History has shown that judicial appointees sometimes stray over time from their initial ideological stances.[181] Examples abound of justices appointed by Republican presidents who once cherished "common sense"[182] but then strayed from originalism. Curiously, it never seems that a living constitutionalist judge shifts to originalist thinking!

Still, while a great ideological divide exists in our judiciary, the truth is that on many issues there is common ground. Furthermore, even the staunchest originalist understands that in a real sense the Constitution is a "living, breathing, document"—it is flexible and various judge made "tests" are essential to its continued viability. The core meanings protecting individual liberties must always remain

---

2018, 1:04 PM), https://nypost.com/2018/11/10/why-republicans-actually-have-the-upper-hand-after-the-midterms/.

[180] *See* Alex Swoyer, *Brett Kavanaugh Best Described as 'Originalist,' Say Legal Scholars*, WASH. TIMES (Sept. 13, 2018), https://www.washingtontimes.com/news/2018/sep/3/brett-kavanaugh-best-described-as-originalist-say-/.

[181] *See* Josh Gerstein, *Gorsuch Swings Against Trump in Deportation Case*, POLITICO (April 17, 2018, 6:26 PM), https://www. politico.com/story/2018/04/17/immigration-ruling-gorsuch-528749.

[182] *'I Will Do Equal Right to the Poor and the Rich': Brett Kavanaugh's Remarks to the Senate Committee*, USA TODAY (Sept. 4, 2018, 7:07 PM), https://www.usatoday.com/story/news/politics/2018/09/04/brett-kavanaugh-supreme-court-nominees-remarks-senate-committee/ 1196833002/. ("In deciding cases, a judge must always keep in mind what Alexander Hamilton said in Federalist 83: 'the rules of legal interpretation are rules of common sense.' ").

inviolate, but there is sometimes common ground. In his opening remarks to the Senate judiciary committee in 2018, now Justice Brett Kavanaugh said, "In deciding cases, a judge must always keep in mind what Alexander Hamilton said in Federalist 83: 'the rules of legal interpretation are rules of common sense.'"[183]

---

[183] *Id.*

Chapter Six

The Trump Travel Ban: First Trump Victory

"SUPREME COURT UPHOLDS TRUMP TRAVEL BAN. Wow!"[184]

– President Donald J. Trump

Largely unsupported by a "do nothing" Congress,[185] President Trump has shown great energy in unabashedly fighting for his policies, particularly when it comes to finding ways to secure America's borders from those who blatantly ignore the law—both the illegal aliens and their supporters in the United States. Recognizing that America's southern border was about as secure as a screen door on a submarine, Trump immediately took steps to secure the border. Not only does the President publicly attack the

---

[184] Donald J. Trump (@realDonaldTrump), TWITTER (June 26, 2018, 7:40 AM), https://twitter.com/realdonaldtrump/status/101162027132 7989760?lang=en. *See also* Josh Gerstein & Ted Hesson, *Supreme Court Upholds Trump's Travel Ban*, POLITICO (June 26, 2018, 2:33 PM), https://www.politico.com/story/2018/06/26/supreme-court-upholds-trumps-travel-ban-673181. In a written statement, the White House noted: "Today's Supreme Court ruling is a tremendous victory for the American People and the Constitution. In this era of worldwide terrorism and extremist movements bent on harming innocent civilians, we must properly vet those coming into our country[.]" *Id.*

[185] *See, e.g.,* Susan Ferrechio, *McConnell Vows Senate Will Block House Funding Bill That Excludes Wall Money*, WASH. EXAMINER (Jan. 2, 2019, 7:51 PM), https://www.washingtonexaminer.com/news/ congress/mcconnell-vows-senate-will-block-house-funding-bill-that-excludes-wall-money; Tom Del Beccaro, *Tom Del Beccaro: Trump Proven Right Again, as Tariff Threat Prompts Mexico to Act Against Illegal Immigration*, Fox News (June 8, 2019), https://www. foxnews.com/opinion/tom-del-beccaro-securing-border.

absurdity of ignoring the fact that for years millions of illegal aliens have been allowed to flood into the nation under both Republican and Democrat administrations, he repeatedly expresses great concern about the real possibility of terrorists entering America through a porous border. Of course, in fighting for his policies the Trump Administration is repeated dragged into federal courts by his political and ideological opponents. Ultimately, given the splintered nature of lower federal court decisions and an insatiable desire to issue injunction after injunction against the Trump Administration these legal challenges always end up in the U.S. Supreme Court for a final ruling.

Trump's first major victory at the U.S. Supreme Court, which was a slim 5-4 split, revealed in no uncertain terms the absolute necessity of securing an originalist majority on the high court. The legal battle involved one of the most controversial issues that Trump faced during the first half of his first term in office—President Trump ordered a limited travel ban targeting travelers to the United States from six Muslim-majority countries.[186] Given then-candidate Trump's occasional lapses into rhetoric about "banning Muslims" from entering the United States, his action to implement a tailored travel ban for a handful of Muslim-majority nations set off a firestorm of debate. The expressed consternation was not so much centered on the black letter legality of the executive order, but more so on questioning

---

[186] Although the Trump Travel Ban was particularly galling for those dissatisfied with the results of the 2016 election, other groups were equally disturbed. *See* JTA & TOI Staff, *Jewish Groups Decry Supreme Court Upholding of Trump Travel Ban*, THE TIMES OF ISR. (June 26, 2018, 8:40 PM), https://www.timesofisrael.com/jewish-groups-decry-supreme-court-upholding-of-trump-travel-ban/ (discussing different Jewish organizations and their response to the travel ban); Andrew Buncombe, *Donald Trump's Muslim Ban Inspires Mass Protests Across the United States Involving Millions of Americans*, INDEP. (Jan. 30, 2017, 3:42 PM), https://www.independent.co.uk/news/world/americas/donald-trump-muslim-ban-protests-us-refugee-immigration-policy-syria-iran-iraq-demonstrations-a7553476.html (demonstrating the widespread dissatisfaction with the Trump travel ban).

the underlying motivations of President Trump. In the minds of some, President Trump's decision to implement a travel ban was wholly "unconstitutional" in violation of the Constitution's Establishment Clause. For certain, the travel ban galvanized both those who maintained a trigger-happy reaction to any unorthodox speech by Trump with those who were outraged at a Commander in Chief who seemingly embraced religious intolerance.[187] The question was thus set: was the Trump move a necessary action to keep the nation safe from the threat of radical Islamic terrorism in the ongoing "War on Terror" or a reflection of a deep-seated hostility and animus towards Muslims, which might render the travel ban unconstitutional?[188]

Over the course of the next seventeen months, the attention—both political and legal—that was devoted to the original travel ban and its subsequent iterations was second only to the main-stream media's never-ending fixation on so-called "Trump/Russia" collusion allegations.[189] After a

---

[187] See Andrew Buncombe, *Donald Trump's Muslim Ban Inspires Mass Protests Across the United States Involving Millions of Americans*, INDEP. (Jan. 30, 2017, 3:42 PM), https://www.independent.co.uk/news/world/americas/donald-trump-muslim-ban-protests-us-refugee-immigration-policy-syria-iran-iraq-demonstrations-a7553476.html.

[188] See President George W. Bush, *Address to the Joint Session of the 107th Congress*, SELECTED SPEECHES OF PRESIDENT GEORGE W. BUSH 2001-2008 (Sept. 20, 2001), *available at* https://georgewbush-whitehouse.archives.gov/infocus/bushrecord/documents/Selected_Speeches_George_W_Bush.pdf (stating that: "Our war on terror begins with al Qaeda, but it does not end there. It will not end until every terrorist group of global reach has been found, stopped and defeated."). *See* Richard W. Stevenson, *President Makes It Clear: Phrase is "War on Terror"*, N.Y. TIMES (Aug. 4, 2005), https://www.nytimes.com/2005/08/04/politics/president-makes-it-clear-phrase-is-war-on-terror.html (quoting George W. Bush's Address at the American Legislative Exchange Council (Aug. 3, 2001)).

[189] See Jennifer Harper, *Media Obsession: 55 Percent of Broadcast News Coverage of Trump Centered on Russia Probe*, WASH. TIMES (June 27, 2017), https://www.washingtontimes.com/news/2017/jun/27/media-obsession-55-percent-of-broadcast-news-cover/ (noting the amount of time spent on the Russia matter compared with other

series of lower court rulings that struck down each of the three versions of the president's travel ban, the United States Supreme Court finally settled the matter on June 26, 2018.[190] In a 5-4 opinion written by Chief Justice John Roberts, the majority rejected the challengers' claims of illegality.[191] While fully acknowledging that President Trump had made a series of derogatory and confusing statements about Muslims and a Muslim-ban, the chief justice ruled that the Court "must consider not only the statements of a particular president, but also the authority of the presidency itself."[192] In other words, for the originalist members of the Court the question revolved around "the significance of those statements in reviewing a presidential directive, neutral on its face, addressing a matter within the core of executive responsibility."[193]

According to the Court the sole prerequisite behind the face of the government's action requires only that the executive present an explanation for the travel ban that is "plausibly related" to a legitimate national security objective.[194] Thus, since the text of the travel ban said

important policy topics); *See also* Ed Rogers, *The Media's Mass Hysteria Over 'Collusion' is Out of Control*, WASH. POST (July 11, 2017), https://www.washingtonpost.com/blogs/post-partisan/wp/2017/07/11/the-medias-mass-hysteria-over-collusion-is-out-of-control/?noredirect=on&utm_term=.c3a32fa5ed8a (pointing to different news stations like *New York Times* and *Politico* to demonstrate the "breathless coverage."); *The Media's Unhealthy Trump-Russia Obsession . . . By the Numbers*, INVESTOR'S BUS. DAILY (June 29, 2017), https://www.investors.com/politics/editorials/the-medias-unhealthy-trump-russia-obsession-by-the-numbers/ (noting an analysis which found, "from May 17 through June 20, the big three networks devoted 353 minutes of their precious airtime to the Russia story—equal to more than half the networks' total Trump coverage over those weeks.").

[190] Trump v. Hawaii, 138 S. Ct. 2392 (2018).

[191] *Id.* at 2402.

[192] *Id.* at 2418.

[193] *Id.* at 2401.

[194] *Id.* at 2420.

nothing about religion, the Court ruled that the travel ban "order was expressly premised on legitimate purposes: preventing entry of nationals who cannot be adequately vetted and inducing other nations to improve their practices."[195] In short, the President of the United States has the absolute constitutional authority to restrict the entry of aliens whenever he finds that their entry "would be detrimental to the interests of the United States," in accordance with the applicable Congressional statute.[196]

The purpose of this chapter is to trace the litigious journey of the Trump travel ban with attention to the efficacy of judicial review over issues related to matters that are outside of the "four corners" of an Executive Branch action related to national security and foreign relations. Again, the final decision demonstrated the critical necessity of having an originalist majority on the high court. In this context, the trip is not solely about assessing the jurisprudence, particularly when opponents of the Trump travel ban relied heavily on then presidential candidate Donald Trump's own inflammatory rhetoric about "banning Muslims" when arguing for relief from the executive order. As plainly cited by the plaintiffs in *Trump v. Hawaii*, there is no question that President Trump's untoward pronouncements, which smack of religious discrimination, saddled the Trump presidency with a whole host of negative connotations causing ample ground for concern.[197] While President Trump's personal oratory sometimes runs counter to the otherwise laudable core meaning of his signature phrase, "Make America Great Again," religious bias is absolutely *anathema* to the American ethos and the establishment pillars.[198]

---

[195] *Id.* at 2421.

[196] 8 U.S.C. § 1182(f) (2012).

[197] *Trump*, 138 S. Ct. at 2417 (2018).

[198] Pamela Engel, *How Trump Came Up with His Slogan 'Make America Great Again'*, BUS. INSIDER, (Jan. 18, 2017, 10:15 AM), http://www.businessinsider.com/trump-make-america-great-again-slogan-history-2017-1.

Apart from President Trump's well-established penchant for hyperbolic monologue, evaluating the Trump travel ban in an objective manner is fraught with other built-in difficulties. As noted, in the prologue to this book the American people are exposed to a relentless drumbeat of anti-Trump vitriol both from his political opponents, but also from a very vocal and partisan main-stream media,[199] where almost every action or pronouncement by President Trump is treated with open suspicion and viperous contempt.[200]

---

[199] *See* Charles M. Blow, *Soul Survival in Trump's Hell*, N.Y. TIMES (Sept. 11, 2017), https://www.nytimes.com/2017/09/11/opinion/soul-survival-in-trumps-hell.html (arguing that living in the Trump Administration is the equivalent of existing in a living hell); *see also* Howard Kurtz, *Behind the Vitriol: Are Trump's Critics Mimicking his Tactics?*, FOX NEWS (April 26, 2018), http://www.foxnews.com/politics/2018/04/26/behind-vitriol-are-trumps-critics-mimicking-his-tactics.html (examining the media's coverage of the Trump Administration); Jeremy W. Peters, *As Critics Assail Trump, his Supporters Dig in Deeper*, N.Y. TIMES (June 23, 2018), https://www.nytimes.com/2018/06/23/us/politics/republican-voters-trump.html (discussing the harsh responses to President Trump's decisions).

[200] *See* Stephen Dinan, *Networks' Coverage of Trump Immigration Policy 92 Percent Negative*, WASH. TIMES (July 24, 2018), https://www.washingtontimes.com/news/2018/jul/24/networks-coverage-trump-immigration-policy-92-perc/ (demonstrating staggering negativity across ABC, CBS, and NBC towards Trump's immigration policy); Tom Engelhardt, *The Media Have a Trump Addiction*, THE NATION (Mar. 27, 2018), https://www.thenation.com/article/the-media-has-a-trump-addiction/ (exhibiting the historic amount of media coverage of President Trump: "no human being in history has ever been covered in this fashion[.]"). Jennifer Harper, *Numbers Don't Lie: Media Coverage Against Trump is Entrenched, Vicious, Persistent*, WASH. TIMES (June 29, 2017), https://www.washingtontimes.com/news/2017/jun/29/inside-the-beltway-media-bias-against-trump-is-ent/; *see also* Jennifer Harper, *Unprecedented Hostility: Broadcast Coverage of President Trump Still 90% Negative, Says Study*, WASH. TIMES (Mar. 6, 2018), https://www.washingtontimes.com/news/2018/mar/6/trump-coverage-still-90-negative-says-new-study/ ("Out of a total of 712 evaluative comments made on the air, only 65 were positive, or 9 percent. The rest—647 comments—were negative, amounting to 91 percent."). *See also* Deborah Howell, *An Obama Tilt in Campaign Coverage*, WASH. POST (Nov. 9, 2008),

Both realities, Trump's penchant for offensive phrases and the media's bias, play loudly in entertaining open and rational discussions on even the most basic of issues.

– Living Constitutionalist Judges Challenge the Trump Travel Ban –

As the Republican Party's chosen candidate during the 2016 presidential contest, Donald Trump expressed pointed dissatisfaction with a number of policies, practices, and people in a manner that left many observers highly unsettled—both in terms of Trump's occasional lack of common civility and unconventional content.[201] However unartfully articulated on the long campaign trail, candidate Trump was especially keen on speaking out about securing and controlling America's wide-open borders.[202] Some of his justifications centered on the inherent right of any sovereign nation to ensure border integrity by requiring foreigners seeking admission to follow lawful immigration laws, but Trump also cited national security threats as a reason for restricting those seeking entrance into the

---

http://www.washingtonpost.com/wp-dyn/content/article/2008/11/07/AR2008110702895.html (admitting that there was a distinct media slant towards Obama during the then presidential campaign and citing the number of positive stories about Obama versus the number of positive stories about McCain); Thomas E. Patterson, *News Coverage of Donald Trump's First 100 Days* (HKS Faculty Research Working Paper, Series 10, RWP17-040, Sept. 2017) ("Trump's coverage during his first 100 days was not merely negative in overall terms. It was unfavorable on every dimension. There was not a single major topic where Trump's coverage was more positive than negative.").

[201] Sarah McCammon, *Donald Trump has Brought on Countless Controversies in an Unlikely Campaign*, NPR (Nov. 5, 2016), https://www.npr.org/2016/11/05/500782887/donald-trumps-road-to-election-day.

[202] *A History of Trump's Border Wall*, COUNTABLE (Apr. 25, 2017), https://www.countable.us/articles/418-history-trump-s-border-wall.

country.[203] Thus, he touted building a more robust physical wall along the Mexico border as well as targeting other types of immigrants to include those allowed into the nation on a temporary protected status[204] and the Obama created Deferred Action for Childhood Arrivals (DACA).[205] In terms of national security threats to the nation, Trump's greatest concern was centered on protecting the United States from the very real threat of radical Islamic terrorism,[206] particularly given the backdrop of horrendous ISIS[207] inspired terror attacks in the West during the 2014-2016 timeframe.[208]

---

[203] *See* Donald J. Trump, Donald Trump's Immigration Speech in Phx., Ariz. (Aug. 31, 2016) (transcript available at https://www.nytimes.com/2016/09/02/us/politics/transcript-trump-immigration-speech.html); Ron Nixon & Linda Qiu, *Trump's Evolving Words on the Wall*, N.Y. TIMES (Jan. 18, 2018), https://www.nytimes.com/2018/01/18/us/politics/trump-border-wall-immigration.html.

[204] *See* Maya Rhodan, *Trump Looks to End Temporary Status for Some Immigrants*, TIME (Nov. 20, 2017), https://www.scribd.com/article/364096365/Trump-Looks-To-End-Temporary-Status-For-Some-Immigrants (reporting on the Department of Homeland Security's intention to end temporary protected status in early 2019 for 2,500 immigrants who came to the U.S. from Nicaragua in 1998 after Hurricane Mitch).

[205] The Trump Administration rescinded DACA in September 2017. *See* DEP'T OF HOMELAND SEC., MEMORANDUM ON RESCISSION OF DEFERRED ACTION FOR CHILDHOOD ARRIVALS ("DACA") (Sept. 5, 2017), ("This memorandum rescinds the June 15, 2012 memorandum entitled 'Exercising Prosecutorial Discretion with Respect to Individuals Who Came to the United States as Children,' which established the program known as Deferred Action for Childhood Arrivals.").

[206] Masood Farivar, *Trump Pledges War on Radical Islamic Terrorism*, VOA NEWS (Jan. 18, 2017, 8:27 AM), https://www.voanews.com/a/donald-trump-pledges-war-radical-islamic-terrorism/3676303.html.

[207] *ISIS Fast Facts*, CNN (Sept. 3, 2018), https://www.cnn.com/2014/08/08/world/isis-fast-facts/index.html.

[208] John Haltiwanger, *ISIS in America: How Many Times Has the Islamic State Attacked the U.S.?*, NEWSWEEK (Dec. 11, 2017), https://www.newsweek.com/islamic-state-america-attacks-744497

Indeed, on January 27, 2017, one week after taking the oath of office, President Trump issued Executive Order No. 13769 (Travel Ban EO-1),[209] a temporary travel ban[210] for individuals seeking entrance into the United States from seven Muslim-majority countries that "had been previously identified by Congress or prior administrations as posing heightened terrorism risks."[211] The order was directly focused at longstanding hotbeds of terrorism—Iran, Libya, Somalia, Syria, Sudan, Yemen, and Iraq.[212] Travel Ban EO-1, entitled "Protecting the Nation from Foreign Terrorist Entry Into the United States," also halted the U.S. refugee program for 120 days and suspended all Syrian refugees indefinitely.[213] As the title suggested, Travel Ban EO-1 also directed the Secretary of Homeland Security to conduct a thorough review regarding the adequacy of information provided by foreign governments about their nationals who sought entry into the United States.[214]

Trump's reasoning in selecting the seven nations for a temporary immigration suspension was because each "is a state sponsor of terrorism, has been significantly

---

(giving a general background of terrorist attacks linked to ISIS in the United States).

[209] Exec. Order No. 13,769, 82 Fed. Reg. 8,977 (Jan. 27, 2017).

[210] For an excellent overview of the evolution of the travel bans, *See* HILLER R. SMITH & BEN HARRINGTON, CONG. RESEARCH SERV., LSB10017, LEGAL SIDEBAR: OVERVIEW OF "TRAVEL BAN" LITIGATION AND RECENT DEVELOPMENTS (Apr. 23, 2018), *available at* https://fas.org/sgp/crs/homesec/LSB10017.pdf.

[211] Trump v. Hawaii, 138 S. Ct. 2392, 2403 (2018).

[212] Exec. Order No. 13,769, 82 Fed. Reg. 8,977 (Jan. 27, 2017). President Trump's executive order affects travelers who have a nationality in those seven countries, but those who have dual nationality with a non-restricted country are not affected, so long as they travel on the passport from the other country. *Trump's executive order: Who Does the Travel Ban Affect*, BBC NEWS (Feb. 10, 2017), http://www.bbc.com/news/world-us-canada-38781302.

[213] Exec. Order No. 13769, 82 Fed. Reg. 8,977 (Jan. 27, 2017).

[214] *Id.*

compromised by terrorist organizations, or contains active conflict zones."[215] Further, not only were all the listed countries rife with radical Islamic extremists, but many of them also possessed a governmental bureaucracy that had little or no credibility in terms of identifying with precision the identity of people seeking visas to enter the United States.[216] Although the Trump Administration's justification for the travel ban centered on objective and logical concerns regarding national security and loose vetting practices, his critics voiced other motivations for the issuance of EO-1.[217] Pointing to some of Donald Trump's political campaign rhetoric, opponents complained that EO-1 was actually a guise for "banning Muslims" entrance into the United States.[218] After locating a federal district judge in Washington State that was sympathetic to this theory, it was only a matter of days before Travel Ban EO-1 was blocked[219]

[215] U.S. EMBASSY & CONSULATES IN FRANCE, EXECUTIVE ORDER PROTECTING THE NATION FROM FOREIGN TERRORIST ENTRY INTO THE UNITED STATES (Mar. 6, 2017), https://fr.usembassy.gov/executive-order-protecting-nation-foreign-terrorist-entry-united-states/.

[216] Donald Trump implemented the ban on visa issuance until the Department of Homeland Security could improve its vetting system to properly exclude jihadist-infiltrators within the refugee flow. *Trump Expected to Sign Executive Orders on Immigration,* CNBC (Jan. 24, 2017, 6:36 PM), https://www.cnbc.com/2017/01/24/trump-to-restrict-immigration-from-several-middle-east-countries-reuters.html.

[217] *See* William Saletan, *Of Course It's a Muslim Ban,* SLATE (Jan. 31, 2017, 1:13 PM), http://www.slate.com/articles/news_and_politics/politics/2017/01/trump_s_executive_order_on_immigration_is_a_muslim_ban.html (arguing Trump's rhetoric clearly indicates his true intentions of banning all Muslims).

[218] *Id.*

[219] Washington v. Trump, No. C17-0141JLR, 2017 WL 462040 (W.D. Wash. Feb. 3, 2017), *appeal dismissed,* No. 17-35105, 2017 WL 3774041 U.S. App. LEXIS 4235 (9th Cir. Mar. 8, 2017). U.S. District Court Judge James Robart found the plaintiffs that filed the lawsuit "have met their burden of demonstrating that they face immediate and irreparable injury as a result of the signing and implementation of the executive order." *Id.* at *6-7. The Trump Travel Ban EO-1 was blocked nationwide. *Id.* at *8.

124

by a universal or "nationwide injunction,"[220] an order which the Ninth Circuit shortly thereafter upheld.[221] In response to the Ninth Circuit's ruling, on March 6, 2017, President Trump revoked Travel Ban EO-1 and replaced it with a new travel ban per Executive Order No. 13780 ("Travel Ban EO-2").[222] The revised Travel Ban EO-2 stated in part:

> Given the foregoing [concerns about Iran, Libya, Somalia, Syria, Sudan, and Yemen], the entry into the United States of foreign nationals who may commit, aid, or support acts of terrorism remains a matter of grave concern. In light of the Ninth Circuit's observation that the political branches are better suited to determine the appropriate scope of any suspensions than are the courts, and in order to avoid spending additional time pursuing litigation, I am revoking Executive Order 13769 [(the original travel-ban)] and replacing it with this order, which expressly excludes from the suspensions categories of aliens that have prompted judicial concerns and which clarifies or refines the approach to certain other issues or categories of affected aliens.
>
> * * * *
>
> To temporarily reduce investigative burdens on relevant agencies during the review period described

---

[220] For an excellent overview of the use of nationwide injunctions by federal courts, *See* WILSON C. FREEMAN, CONG. RESEARCH SERV., LSB10124, LEGAL SIDEBAR: THE TRAVEL BAN CASE AND NATIONWIDE INJUNCTIONS (May 2, 2018), *available at* https://fas.org/sgp/crs/homesec/LSB10124.pdf.

[221] Washington v. Trump, 847 F.3d 1151 (9th Cir. 2017) (per curium).

[222] *See* Exec. Order No. 13,780, 82 Fed. Reg. 13,209 (Mar. 6, 2017) (revoking Executive Order 13,769—the original travel ban). President Trump was less than satisfied with this revised version of the travel ban, calling it a "watered down, politically correct version" of the prior executive order. Louis Nelson, *Trump Slams Justice Department for 'Watered Down' Travel Ban*, POLITICO (June 5, 2017, 7:17 AM), https://www.politico.com/story/2017/06/05/trump-travel-ban-justice-department-239131.

in subsection (a) of this section, to ensure the proper review and maximum utilization of available resources for the screening and vetting of foreign nationals, to ensure that adequate standards are established to prevent infiltration by foreign terrorists, and in light of the national security concerns referenced in section 1 of this order, I hereby proclaim, pursuant to sections 212(f) and 215(a) of the INA, 8 U.S.C. 1182(f) and 1185(a), that the unrestricted entry into the United States of nationals of Iran, Libya, Somalia, Sudan, Syria, and Yemen would be detrimental to the interests of the United States. I therefore direct that the entry into the United States of nationals of those six countries be suspended for 90 days from the effective date of this order, subject to the limitations, waivers, and exceptions set forth in sections 3 and 12 of this order.[223]

---

[223] Exec. Order No. 13,780, 82 Fed. Reg. 13,209 (Mar. 6, 2017). Iraq, a U.S. ally, was removed from the original Trump Travel Ban EO-1 due to the Iraqi government's concerted effort in combating ISIS and stabilizing the region. The executive order stated:

Iraq presents a special case. Portions of Iraq remain active combat zones. Since 2014, ISIS has had dominant influence over significant territory in northern and central Iraq. Although that influence has been significantly reduced due to the efforts and sacrifices of the Iraqi government and armed forces, working along with a United States-led coalition, the ongoing conflict has impacted the Iraqi government's capacity to secure its borders and to identify fraudulent travel documents. Nevertheless, the close cooperative relationship between the United States and the democratically elected Iraqi government, the strong United States diplomatic presence in Iraq, the significant presence of United States forces in Iraq, and Iraq's commitment to combat ISIS justify different treatment for Iraq. In particular, those Iraqi government forces that have fought to regain more than half of the territory previously dominated by ISIS have shown steadfast determination and earned enduring respect as they battle an armed group that is the common enemy of Iraq and the United States. In addition, since Executive Order 13769 was issued, the Iraqi government has expressly

1

Despite the Trump Administration's measured changes set out in the revised Travel Ban EO-2, opponents were not satiated, and the legal challenges immediately resumed.[224] Detractors were in no way impressed with the ramification of Travel Ban EO-2 vis a vis Muslims and continued to cite President Trump's campaign speeches about anti-Muslim animus as proof of his "real intent" on the matter, which they viewed as overt religious discrimination in violation of the Establishment Clause.[225] Predictably, it did not take long

---

undertaken steps to enhance travel documentation, information sharing, and the return of Iraqi nationals' subject to final orders of removal. Decisions about issuance of visas or granting admission to Iraqi nationals should be subjected to additional scrutiny to determine if applicants have connections with ISIS or other terrorist organizations, or otherwise pose a risk to either national security or public safety.

Id. The order also exempted current visa holders and permanent residents from the travel ban. The ban on Syrian refugees remained but was changed to 120 days instead of indefinitely. *Id.*

[224] *See* Naureen Shah, *Trump's Muslim Ban 2.0 Is Just as Inhumane— and Even More Frightening*, TIME (Mar. 6, 2017), http://time. com/4692814/trump-travel-ban-muslims/; Alexander Burns, *2 Federal Judges Rules Against Trump's Latest Travel Ban*, N.Y. TIMES (March 15, 2017), https://www.nytimes.com/2017/03/15/us/politics/trump-travel-ban.html.

[225] The Establishment Clause is contained in the First Amendment to the U.S. Constitution and provides, in part, that "Congress shall make no law respecting an establishment of religion, or prohibiting the free exercise thereof[.]" U.S. CONST. amend. I. *See* Alexander Burns, *2 Federal Judges Rules Against Trump's Latest Travel Ban*, N.Y. TIMES (March 15, 2017), https://www.nytimes.com/2017/03/15/us/politics/ trump-travel-ban.html (citing some of President Trump's campaign documents which called for a total shutdown of all Muslims entering the United States); Kaitlyn Schallhorn, *Trump Travel Ban: Timeline of a Legal Journey*, FOX NEWS (Oct. 10, 2017), http://www.foxnews. com/politics/2017/07/19/trump-travel-ban-timeline-legal-journey.html (arguing that the travel bans have little to do with national security and has more resemblance to furtherance to President Trump's "promised Muslim ban"); Naureen Shah, *Trump's Muslim Ban 2.0 Is Just as Inhumane—and Even More Frightening*, TIME (Mar. 6, 2017), http://time.com/4692814/trump-travel-ban-muslims/ (arguing that those who disagree with the travel ban consider it an irrational misnomer

before the President's new Travel Ban EO-2 was once again blocked by means of another universal injunction, this time by federal district courts in Maryland[226] and Hawaii.[227] On the Government's appeal of the Maryland district court's ruling, the Fourth Circuit made its concerns clear when it refused to allow Travel Ban EO-2 to take effect.[228] The Fourth Circuit's opinion upholding the lower court injunction was rubricated with numerous quotes from then-candidate Donald Trump.[229] The Appellate court stated:

> On December 7, 2015, then-candidate Trump published a "Statement on Preventing Muslim Immigration" on his campaign website, which proposed, "a total and complete shutdown of Muslims entering the United States until our country's representatives can figure out what is going on." That same day, he highlighted the statement on Twitter, "Just put out a very important policy statement on the extraordinary influx of hatred & danger coming into our country. We must be vigilant!" And Trump read from the statement at a campaign rally in Mount Pleasant, South Carolina, that evening, where he remarked, "I have friends that are Muslims. They are great people—but they know we have a problem."

which directly hurts the country by refusing to admit refugees). *See also* David B. Rivkin Jr. & Lee A. Casey, *The Fourth Circuit Joins the 'Resistance'*, WALL ST. J., (May 29, 2017, 11:30 AM), https://www.wsj.com/articles/the-fourth-circuit-joins-the-resistance-1496071859 (arguing that making foreign policy is not the job of the courts).

[226] Int'l Refugee Assistance Project v. Trump, 241 F. Supp. 3d 539 (D. Md. 2017), *aff'd in part, vacated in part*, 857 F.3d 554 (4th Cir. 2017), *cert. granted*, 137 S. Ct. 2080 (2017), *vacated*, 138 S. Ct. 353 (2017).

[227] Hawai'i v. Trump, 241 F. Supp. 3d 1119 (D. Haw. 2017).

[228] Int'l Refugee Assistance Project v. Trump, 857 F.3d 554 (4th Cir. 2017), *cert. granted*, 137 S. Ct. 2080 (2017), *vacated*, 138 S. Ct. 353 (2017).

[229] *Id.* at 575-76.

In an interview with CNN on March 9, 2016, Trump professed, "I think Islam hates us," and we can't allow people coming into the country who have this hatred." Katrina Pierson, a Trump spokeswoman, told CNN "we've allowed this propaganda to spread all through the country that Islam is a religion of peace." In a March 22, 2016 interview with Fox Business television, Trump reiterated his call for a ban on Muslim immigration, claiming that this proposed ban had received "tremendous support" and stating, "We're having problems with the Muslims, and we're having problems with Muslims coming into the country." "You need surveillance," Trump explained, and "you have to deal with the mosques whether you like it or not."[230]

The Trump Administration sought immediate relief from the Fourth Circuit's findings at the United States Supreme Court. In a consolidated ruling issued in June 2017, the Court stayed the decisions of all lower courts and allowed Trump's revised Travel Ban EO-2 to implement with minor adjustments, pending the Court's full review on the merits.[231] In summation, the Court held that Travel Ban EO-2 could be enforced against travelers from the six named countries if the traveler lacked a "credible claim of a bona fide relationship with a person or entity in the United States."[232]

Undaunted by this setback, opponents subsequently sought clarification from the Hawaiian federal district court on the Court's ruling with particular attention to the meaning of the term "bona fide relationship."[233] In quickstep, the

---

[230] *Id.* (footnote omitted).

[231] Trump v. Int'l Refugee Assistance Project, 137 S. Ct. 2080 (2017) (per curium).

[232] *Id.* at 2088.

[233] Initially, the federal district court sitting in Hawaii refused to clarify anything, stating "Plaintiffs' request for [emergency] clarification is DENIED without prejudice to its re-filing with the Supreme Court."

Hawaiian district court modified the scope of the revised Travel Ban EO-2 to include exceptions for grandparents and other relatives from the prohibited countries if they had a "bona fide relationship" with a person(s) in the United States.[234] The Hawaiian district court also found that "refugees with formal assurances from government-contracted resettlement agencies"[235] also had the required bona fide relationship to be protected. The Ninth Circuit upheld the Hawaiian district court's modification in full.[236]

Ironically, on the 16th anniversary of the terror attacks of September 11, 2001,[237] the Supreme Court issued a temporary stay of the new lower federal court actions, allowing the primary thrust of the Trump Travel Ban EO-2 to proceed until the Court could take up the full matter on October 10, 2017.[238] Without dissent, Justice Kennedy stated:

> UPON CONSIDERATION of the application of counsel for the applicants, IT IS ORDERED that the mandate of the United States Court of Appeals for the Ninth Circuit, case No. 17-16426, is hereby stayed with respect to refugees covered by a formal assurance, pending receipt of a response, due on or

Hawai'i v. Trump, 258 F. Supp. 3d 1188, 1191 (D. Haw. 2017) (footnote omitted), *appeal dismissed*, 863 F.3d 1102 (9th Cir. 2017).

[234] State v. Trump, 263 F. Supp. 3d 1049, 1057-58 (D. Haw. 2017), *aff'd*, 871 F.3d 646 (9th Cir. 2017).

[235] *Id.* at 1059-60.

[236] *See generally* State v. Trump, 871 F.3d 646 (9th Cir. 2017).

[237] Anne Gearan, *At White House and Pentagon, Trump Marks 16th Anniversary of Sept. 11 Attacks*, WASH. POST (Sept. 11, 2017), https://www.washingtonpost.com/news/post-politics/wp/2017/09/11/trump-marks-16th-anniversary-of-sept-11-attacks-at-white-house-ceremony/?noredirect=on&utm_term=.3b373df5b01f.

[238] Trump v. Hawaii, 138 S. Ct. 1, 1 (2017).

before Tuesday, September 12, 2017, by 12 p.m., and further order of the undersigned or of the Court.[239]

On September 24, 2017, as opponents were still preparing their initial arguments to the Court, the Trump Administration issued Presidential Proclamation 9645, "Enhancing Vetting Capabilities and Processes for Detecting Attempted Entry Into the United States by Terrorists or Other Public-Safety Threats" (Travel Ban EO-3).[240] Travel Ban EO-3 somewhat refocused the previous Travel Ban EO-2, but more importantly had the effect of derailing the entire case set for adjudication before the Court.[241] The Trump Administration had simply allowed

---

[239] *Id.*

[240] *See* Proclamation No. 9645, 82 Fed. Reg. 45,161 (Sept. 24, 2017).

[241] The issuance of Proclamation 9645 came on the very day the March travel-ban expired—September 24, 2017. Proclamation 9645 stated:

> In Executive Order 13780 of March 6, 2017 (Protecting the Nation from Foreign Terrorist Entry into the United States), on the recommendations of the Secretary of Homeland Security and the Attorney General, I ordered a worldwide review of whether, and if so what, additional information would be needed from each foreign country to assess adequately whether their nationals seeking to enter the United States pose a security or safety threat.

> Despite those efforts, the Secretary of Homeland Security, in consultation with the Secretary of State and the Attorney General, has determined that a small number of countries—out of nearly 200 evaluated—remain deficient at this time with respect to their identity-management and information-sharing capabilities, protocols, and practices. In some cases, these countries also have a significant terrorist presence within their territory.

> * * * *

> After reviewing the Secretary of Homeland Security's report of September 15, 2017, and accounting for the foreign policy, national security, and counterterrorism objectives of the United States, I have determined to restrict and limit the entry of nationals of 7 countries found to be "inadequate" with respect to the baseline described in subsection (c) of this section: Chad, Iran, Libya, North Korea, Syria, Venezuela, and Yemen. These

Travel Ban EO-2 to expire and Trump's new Travel Ban EO-3 would now serve as the latest and final travel ban. Under Travel Ban EO-3, which had no expiration date, Sudan was removed from the EO-2 list of restricted countries, while three non-Muslim majority countries, North Korea, Venezuela, and Chad were added.[242]   The next day, September 25, 2017, the Supreme Court announced that it was removing the Travel Ban EO-2 case from its scheduled docket in order to determine if the new Travel Ban EO-3 had rendered the matter of Travel Ban EO-2 moot as a "live case or controversy."[243]   After considering the legal briefs from

---

restrictions distinguish between the entry of immigrants and nonimmigrants. Persons admitted on immigrant visas become lawful permanent residents of the United States. Such persons may present national security or public-safety concerns that may be distinct from those admitted as nonimmigrants.

* * * *

The Secretary of Homeland Security determined that Somalia generally satisfies the information-sharing requirements of the baseline described in subsection (c) of this section, but its government's inability to effectively and consistently cooperate, combined with the terrorist threat that emanates from its territory, present special circumstances that warrant restrictions and limitations on the entry of its nationals into the United States. Somalia's identity-management deficiencies and the significant terrorist presence within its territory make it a source of particular risks to the national security and public safety of the United States. Based on the considerations mentioned above, and as described further in section 2(h) of this proclamation, I have determined that entry restrictions, limitations, and other measures designed to ensure proper screening and vetting for nationals of Somalia are necessary for the security and welfare of the United States.

Proclamation No. 9645, 82 Fed. Reg. 45161 (Sept. 24, 2017).

[242] *Id.*

[243] *See* Trump v. Int'l Refugee Assistance Project, 138 S. Ct. 50 (2017) (mem.) (The Court's order directed the parties to file briefs concerning the issuance of the new travel ban policy and whether the issue before the court had been rendered moot). The order suggested that the Court was "contemplating dismissing the case and leaving the challengers to press their arguments at a federal trial court." Greg Stohr, *Supreme*

both sides, the Supreme Court dropped the plaintiff's case against Travel Ban EO-2 on October 10, 2017, expressing no views on the merits.[244] In an 8-1 opinion, the Court stated:

> We granted certiorari in this case to resolve a challenge to "the temporary suspension of entry of aliens abroad under Section 2(c) of Executive Order No. 13780." Because that provision of the Order "expired by its own terms" on September 24, 2017, the appeal no longer presents a "live case or controversy." Following our established practice in such cases, the judgment is therefore vacated, and the case is remanded to the United States Court of Appeals for the Fourth Circuit with instructions to dismiss as moot the challenge to Executive Order No. 13780. We express no view on the merits.[245]

Although the Supreme Court had seemingly avoided what would clearly have been viewed as a politically charged decision, they were sadly mistaken. New plaintiffs—"the State of Hawaii, three individuals with foreign relatives affected by the entry suspension, and the Muslim Association of Hawaii"[246]—quickly filed suit in the same federal district court that had heard the previous challenge to Travel Ban EO-2, and the same objections were

Court Drops Travel Ban Argument After Trump Revises Policy, BLOOMBERG (Sept. 25, 2017, 12:39 PM), http://www.bloomberg.com/ news/articles/2017-09-25/supreme-court-drops-travel-ban-case-from-argument-schedule-j80gj8qj.

[244] *See generally* Trump v. Int'l Refugee Assistance Project, 138 S. Ct. 353 (2017) (mem.).

[245] *Id.* (citations omitted). On October 23, 2017, the Supreme Court had also vacated the original decision under appeal from the Ninth Circuit, which derails any new attempts to use that appellate court decision as precedent. *See generally* Trump v. Hawaii, 138 S. Ct. 377 (2017) (mem.); Adam Liptak, *Supreme Court Wipes Out Travel Ban Appeal*, N.Y. TIMES (Oct 24, 2017), https://www.nytimes.com /2017/10/24/us/politics/supreme-court-travel-ban-appeal-trump.html.

[246] Trump v. Hawaii, 138 S. Ct. 2392, 2418 (2018).

made. Predictably, the plaintiffs argued that the new Travel Ban EO-3 was still nothing more than a "Muslim ban" in disguise[247] and violated two specific provisions of the Immigration and Nationality Act ("INA"),[248] as well as the Establishment Clause of the First Amendment.[249] Hawaii federal district judge Derrick Watson agreed with the plaintiffs and once again ordered a nationwide injunction to block Travel Ban EO-3 from taking effect.[250] In turn, the Trump Administration requested expedited briefing and a stay of the nationwide injunction to the Court of Appeals for the Ninth Circuit.[251] In granting a partial stay of the injunction,[252] the Ninth Circuit did not evaluate the Establishment Clause claim, but affirmed the district court's holding that Travel Ban EO-3 violated two specific provisions of the Immigration and Nationality Act (INA)— Section 1182(f) and Section 1152(a)(1)(A).[253]

After reviewing the Ninth Circuit's ruling upholding the temporary injunction, the Supreme Court once again ruled in favor of the Trump Administration when it voted 7-2 in early December 2017, that the new Travel Ban EO-3 could take

---

[247] *See* Richard Wolf & Adam Gomez, *Federal Judge in Hawaii Blocks Trump's Third Travel Ban*, USA TODAY (Oct. 18, 2017), https://www.usatoday.com/story/news/politics/2017/10/17/federal-judge-hawaii-strikes-down-trumps-third-travel-ban/773074001/ (citing Hawaii district federal Judge Derrick Watson's ruling which claimed that the new travel-ban "suffers from precisely the same maladies as its predecessor"). *See also* Richard Wolf, *Children of Japanese American Legal pioneers from World War II Fight Travel Ban*, USA TODAY (Oct. 11, 2017), https://www.usatoday.com/story/news/politics/2017/10/10/children-japanese-american-legal-pioneers-world-war-ii-fight-travel-ban/740910001/.

[248] *See* SMITH & BEN HARRINGTON, note 220, at 5.

[249] *Id.* at 6.

[250] *See generally* Hawaii v. Trump, 878 F.3d 662, 702 (9th Cir. 2017), *rev'd*, 138 S. Ct. 2392, U.S. 2392, 2423 (2017).

[251] *Id.* at 675.

[252] *Id.* at 702.

[253] *Id.* at 694, 697, 702.

full effect pending the government's appeal on the merits of the case.[254] Finally, six months later, on June 26, 2018, the full Court made a final determination on the merits of Trump's Travel Ban EO-3.[255]

In a 5-4 decision, the Court reversed the lower court's "grant of the preliminary injunction as an abuse of discretion" and remanded the case "for further proceeding consistent with" their opinion.[256] In short, citing an impressive string of long-standing case law and employing the Court's "rational basis scrutiny" standard of review,[257] Travel Ban EO-3 was deemed Constitutional, handing President Donald J. Trump his first major judicial victory. Chief Justice John Roberts penned the decision.

– Overview of *Trump vs. Hawaii* –

Signaling from the very beginning of its lengthy opinion that the Court was going to concentrate almost exclusively on the precise wording and related working history of Travel Ban EO-3 rather than on President Trump's offensive remarks about Muslims, Chief Justice Roberts was nevertheless meticulous in addressing the various challenges made by the plaintiffs to include their Establishment Clause claim.[258] Accordingly, the Court heavily colored its opinion upholding Travel Ban EO-3 by outlining the detailed processes and steps taken by the Trump Administration in

---

[254] Trump v. Hawaii, 138 S. Ct. 542 (2017) (mem.); Lawrence Hurley, *U.S. Top Court Lets Trump's Latest Travel Ban Go into Full Effect*, REUTERS (Dec. 4, 2017), https://www.msn.com/en-us/news/us/us-top-court-lets-trumps-latest-travel-ban-go-into-full-effect/ar-BBGexik?li=BBnb7Kz.

[255] Trump v. Hawaii, 138 S. Ct. 2392 (2018).

[256] *Id.* at 2423.

[257] *Id.* at 2420.

[258] *See id.* at 2403 ("We now decide whether the President had authority under the Act to issue the Proclamation, and whether the entry policy violates the Establishment Clause of the First Amendment.").

the terms of the actual mechanics of Proclamation 9645.[259] The Court next dismantled the two textual challenges of the plaintiffs to show definitively that Travel Ban EO-3 did not conflict with the plain language of the INA, which granted the Executive broad enforcement powers to be wielded in his sole discretion.[260] In doing so, the Court also addressed external challenges aimed at the statutory structure and legislative purpose of the INA.[261] Finally, the Court addressed the heart of the matter raised by the plaintiffs that EO-3 was nothing more than a pretext for a Muslim ban that stemmed solely from President Trump's discriminatory attitude toward the religion of Islam.[262]

To show that Travel Ban EO-3 was premised on legitimate purposes, to ensure that certain foreign nationals satisfied the numerous lawful requirements for entry into the United States, the Court first looked squarely at the wording of the primary statutory authority, the INA.[263] The INA provides numerous grounds for restricting aliens entry into the United States as well as making them ineligible for a temporary visa. Containing provisions restricting entry based on health-related grounds,[264] criminal history grounds,[265] terrorist activity grounds,[266] and foreign policy grounds,[267] the Congress has in addition delegated to the

---

[259] *See id.* at 2403–09 (finding each step taken pursuant to Proclamation 9645 " 'craft[ed] . . . country-specific restrictions that would be most likely to encourage cooperation given each country's distinct circumstances,' while securing the Nation until such improvements occur"). *Id.* at 2409.

[260] *Id.* at 2408–10.

[261] *Id.* at 2410–15.

[262] *Id.* at 2416–23.

[263] 8 U.S.C. § 1182 (2012).

[264] § 1182(a)(1).

[265] § 1182(a)(2).

[266] § 1182(a)(3)(B).

[267] § 1182(a)(3)(C).

President the absolute authority under his sole discretion to restrict the entry of aliens on other grounds such as whenever he concluded that their entry "would be detrimental to the interests of the United States."[268] The key text of INA at §1182(f) clearly empowers the President to take unilateral action:

> Whenever the President finds that the entry of any aliens or of any class of aliens into the United States would be detrimental to the interests of the United States, he may by proclamation, and for such period as he shall deem necessary, suspend the entry of all aliens or any class of aliens as immigrants or nonimmigrants, or impose on the entry of aliens any restrictions he may deem to be appropriate.[269]

Given that the sole prerequisite for exercising such board authority *vis a vis* "aliens or of any class of aliens" rests in the President making a finding that admission of such individuals "would be detrimental to the interests of the United States,"[270] EO-3 was firmly set in this grant of power. Under this view, Travel Ban EO-3 was specifically enacted by the Executive Branch to impose entry restrictions on nationals from countries that the President determined did not adequately share information to make an informed entry decision, or that would otherwise pose a threat to national security.[271] Recognizing the deficiencies in gathering the necessary information needed to determine whether nationals of particular countries posed a threat to the public safety of Americans, section 1(a) of Travel Ban EO-3 asserted:

> It is the policy of the United States to protect its citizens from terrorist attacks and other public-safety threats. Screening and vetting protocols and

---

[268] § 1182(f). *See also* Trump v. Hawaii, 138 S. Ct. 2392, 2403 (2017).

[269] *Trump*, 138 S. Ct. at 2408.

[270] *Id.*

[271] Proclamation No. 9645, 82 Fed. Reg. 45,161 (Sept. 27, 2017).

procedures associated with visa adjudications and other immigration processes play a critical role in implementing that policy. They enhance our ability to detect foreign nationals who may commit, aid, or support acts of terrorism, or otherwise pose a safety threat, and they aid our efforts to prevent such individuals from entering the United States.[272]

The Court gave strong note to the fact that Travel Ban EO-3 was premised on a worldwide review of how all States might satisfy the goal of ensuring compliance with fixed security concerns.[273] Included in that review process that was headed by the Department of Homeland Security (DHS), were the Department of State (DOS) and the Director of National Intelligence (DNI).[274] This triad developed a "baseline" of information required from foreign States "to confirm the identity of individuals seeking entry into the United States, and to determine whether those individuals pose a security threat."[275]

The required baseline for evaluation of adequacy was comprised of three separate components.[276] The first, "identity-management information," focused on the integrity of travel documents issued by a foreign country:

> The United States expects foreign governments to provide information about whether persons who seek entry to this country pose national security or public-safety risks. The criteria assessed in this category include whether the country makes available,

---

[272] *Id.* at 45,162.

[273] *Trump*, 138 S. Ct. at 2421.

[274] Homeland Security Act of 2002, Pub. L. No. 107-296, 116 Stat. 2135 (2002) (establishing the Department of Homeland Security in response to the September 11, 2001 terrorist attacks, with the purpose of consolidating the executive branch organizations related to homeland security under one Cabinet level agency).

[275] *Trump*, 138 S. Ct. at 2404.

[276] Proclamation No. 9645, 82 Fed. Reg. at 45, 162–63.

directly or indirectly, known or suspected terrorist and criminal-history information upon request, whether the country impedes the United States Government's receipt of information about passengers and crew traveling to the United States.[277]

The second baseline for evaluation centered on what American agencies considered an acceptable extent to which other countries disclosed information:

The United States expects foreign governments to provide information about whether persons who seek entry to this country pose national security or public-safety risks. The criteria assessed in this category include whether the country makes available, directly or indirectly, known or suspected terrorist and criminal-history information upon request, whether the country provides passport and national-identity document exemplars, and whether the country impedes the United States Government's receipt of information about passengers and crew traveling to the United States.[278]

Finally, the third criteria focused on what agencies assessed in terms of numerous indicators of national security risk:

The national security and public-safety risk assessment category focuses on national security risk indicators. The criteria assessed in this category include whether the country is a known or potential terrorist safe haven, whether it is a participant in the Visa Waiver Program established under section 217 of the INA, 8 U.S.C. 1187, that meets all of its requirements, and whether it fails to receive its nationals subject to final orders of removal from the United States.[279]

---

[277] *Id.* at 45, 162.

[278] *Id.*

[279] *Id.* at 45, 162–63.

When the DHS evaluated all foreign governments against the tiered baseline the Secretary of Homeland Security identified sixteen separate countries as being "inadequate" based on an analysis of their identity-management protocols, information-sharing practices, and other risk factors. Thirty-one additional countries were also classified as "at risk" of becoming inadequate based on those same criteria. The DOS then undertook a "50-day engagement period to encourage all foreign governments" to improve their performance. Resulting from those efforts, numerous countries shared travel documents with DHS and agreed to provide applicable information on known or suspected terrorists.

At the end of the 50-day period, the Secretary of Homeland Security determined that eight countries—Chad, Iran, Iraq, Libya, North Korea, Syria, Venezuela, and Yemen—were deficient and unwilling to share the requested information. Thus, the Secretary of DHS recommended entry restrictions on certain nationals from each of those countries except Iraq, finding that the limitations on Iraqi nationals were not warranted due to the strong and cooperative relationship between the United States and the Iraqi Government to combat ISIS.[280] The Secretary also determined that Somalia, although it generally satisfied the information-sharing component, a deficiency in identity-management coupled with a significant terrorist presence in the country presented special circumstances that warranted further limitations on that nation.[281]

---

[280] *Id.* at 45, 163–64. ISIS is an English abbreviation which stands for *Ad-Dawlah al-Islāmiyah fīl-'Irāq wash-Shām.* ISIS is a Sunni based radical Islamic terror group that originated as a sub-component of al-Qa'eda when Osama Bin Laden franchised his group into Iraq, following the toppling of the regime of Saddam Hussein in 2003 by the United States military. ISIS formally established a caliphate under its leader Abu Bakr AL-Baghdadi in 2014 in parts of Syria and Iraq but has been practically obliterated geographically under the Trump Administration's war policies. *See* ADDICOTT, *supra* note 8, at 232–34.

[281] Proclamation No. 9645, 82 Fed. Reg. 45, 164–65 (Sept. 24, 2017).

After meeting with Cabinet members and considering the results of the review process, the President adopted the recommendations of the Secretary of DHS and issued Travel Ban EO-3.[282] Authorized under the provisions of federal law set out at 8 U.S.C. §§1182(f) and 1185(a), the President determined that entry restrictions were necessary "to prevent the entry of those foreign nationals about whom the United States Government lacks sufficient information[;]" "elicit improved identity management and information sharing protocols and practices from foreign governments;" and to "advance [the] foreign policy, national security, and counterterrorism objectives" of the United States.[283]

– The Plaintiffs' Textual Argument in *Trump v. Hawaii* –

The plaintiffs consisted of the State of Hawaii, three private individuals with foreign relatives affected by Travel Ban EO-3, and the Muslim Association of Hawaii.[284] As stated, they argued that Travel Ban EO-3 violated provisions of the INA as well as the First Amendment's Establishment Clause. In terms of the INA, they asserted that EO-3 directly contravened two provisions of law—§1182(f) and §1152(a)(1)(A). Section 1182(f) authorized the President to "suspend the entry of all aliens or any class of aliens" whenever he "finds" that their entry "would be detrimental to the interests of the United States," and §1152(a)(1)(A) provided that "no person shall . . . be discriminated against in the issuance of an immigrant visa because of the person's race, sex, nationality, place of birth, or place of residence."[285]

Before addressing the merits of the plaintiff's arguments regarding their INA claims, the Court first considered

---

[282] Trump v. Hawaii, 138 S. Ct. 2392, 2405 (2018).

[283] Proclamation No. 9645, 82 Fed. Reg. at 45, 164.

[284] Trump v. Hawaii, 138 S. Ct. at 2406.

[285] *Id.* at 2407, 2413.

whether they had the standing to do so. Relying upon the doctrine of consular non-reviewability, the Government argued that the plaintiffs' challenge to EO-3 was not justiciable under the INA. The Government contended "that because aliens have no 'claim of right' to enter the United States, and because exclusion of aliens is a 'fundamental act of sovereignty' made by the political branches of the State, review of an exclusion decision 'is not within the province of any court, unless expressly authorized by law.'"[286] However, the government failed to argue that the doctrine of consular non-reviewability goes to the Court's subject matter jurisdiction, and it failed to provide any express provision of the INA that directly stripped the Court of its jurisdiction. The Court, therefore, proceeded without deciding whether the plaintiff's claims were reviewable.

As previously noted, the INA not only provides numerous reasons for which an alien abroad may be denied entry into the United States, but also delegates additional direct authority to the President, empowering him to "suspend or restrict the entry of aliens in certain circumstances[,]" particularly under Section 1182(f), which authorizes "the President to 'suspend the entry of all aliens or any class of aliens' whenever he 'finds' that their entry 'would be detrimental to the interests of the United States[.]'"[287] Despite these clear provisions of the INA, the plaintiffs argued that Travel Ban EO-3 was an invalid use of Presidential authority under the INA, contending that §1182(f) only conferred a residual power to temporarily halt the entry of a discrete group of aliens engaged in harmful conduct. The Court rightly disagreed with this view, placing emphasis in its reasoning on the neutral nature of Travel Ban EO-3 as well as the Trump mandated multi-agency review that encompassed all nations, not just Muslim-majority

---

[286] *Id.*

[287] *Id.* (citing 8 U.S.C. §§ 1182(a)(1) (health-related grounds), (a)(2) (criminal history), (a)(3)(B) (terrorist activities), (a)(3)(C) (foreign policy grounds).

nations that took place prior to the order of EO-3. The Court held that:

> By its plain language, §1182(f) grants the President broad discretion to suspend the entry of aliens into the United States. The President lawfully exercised that discretion based on his findings—following a worldwide, multi-agency review—that entry of the covered aliens would be detrimental to the national interest. And Plaintiffs' attempts to identify a conflict with other provisions in the INA, and their appeal to the statute' purposes and legislative history, fail to overcome the clear statutory language.[288]

The Court simply acknowledged what was patently obvious, according to the plain English of the Proclamation. By its own terms, §1182(f) clearly "exudes deference to the President in every clause."[289] Indeed, the Court recognized the only prerequisite in §1182(f) was that the President "find" such an entry "would be detrimental to the interests of the United States."[290] President Trump satisfied that prerequisite based on the multi-agency groundwork and the order for DHS to conduct a worldwide review of every country's cooperation with the "information and risk assessment baseline"[291] established a clear and objective standard that was actually far beyond what the INA would require. In addition, the Court took note that President Trump issued EO-3 only after describing how each country was reviewed utilizing the subject baseline. Only after the review was completed, and at the recommendation of the Secretary of DHS, did the President find "that it was in the national interest to restrict entry of aliens who could not be vetted with adequate information—both to protect national

---

[288] *Id.*

[289] *Id.*

[290] *Id.*

[291] *Id.*

security and public safety, and to induce improvement by their home countries."[292]

Plaintiffs also believed that the findings of the President to support the issuance of Travel Ban EO-3 were inadequate. Specifically, they argued that EO-3 did not give an account for why nationality alone rendered a foreign national a security risk. Plaintiffs further disregarded the President's concern over deficiencies in the vetting process because Travel Ban EO-3 "allows many aliens from the designated countries to enter on nonimmigrant visas."[293] The Court was unconvinced and found that the plaintiffs' arguments were grounded on the incorrect assumption that §1182(f) would require the President to explain his finding in full detail to enable judicial review.[294] Nevertheless, even if the Court had assumed some superior level of scrutiny were proper, the plaintiffs' attacks would still not be sustained. The Court pointed out that the 12-page Travel Ban EO-3 is more detailed than any travel ban order previously issued. Additionally, the Court took little effort in finding that the plaintiffs' request for "inquiry into the persuasiveness of the President's justifications [was] inconsistent with the broad statutory text and the deference traditionally accorded the President in this sphere."[295] The Court was certainly not going to second-guess the President. Asserting long held precedent, the Court stated:

> "Whether the President's chosen method" of addressing perceived risks is justified from a policy perspective is "irrelevant to the scope of his [§1182(f)] authority." And when the President

---

[292] *Id.*

[293] *Id.*

[294] *Id.* (citing Webster v. Doe, 486 U.S. 592, 600 (1988) (concluding that a statute authorizing the CIA Director to terminate an employee when the Director "shall deem such termination necessary or advisable in the interests of the United States" forecloses "any meaningful judicial standard of review.")).

[295] *Id.*

adopts "a preventive measure . . . in the context of international affairs and national security," he is "not required to conclusively link all of the pieces in the puzzle before [courts] grant weight to [his] empirical conclusions."[296]

Finally, the plaintiffs argued that the term "class of aliens" must refer to a definite group of people who share a common "characteristic" distinct from their nationality. Travel Ban EO-3, however, clearly identifies a definite "class of aliens" that is not based on race or religion but on nationality—nationals of select countries—whose entry is suspended. Finding that the text simply did not say what plaintiffs wished it to say, the Court held, "[i]n short, the language of §1182(f) is clear, and the Proclamation [EO-3] does not exceed any textual limit on the President's authority."[297]

– Plaintiffs' Structural & Legislative Purpose Argument –

Unable to logically contend with the "facially broad grant of power"[298] set out in the INA, the plaintiffs' attacked the INA's statutory structure and the legislative purpose. First, they looked for support in the overall immigration scheme set out in the INA as a whole, and then to the legislative history and historical practice of §1182(f). The Court held that neither argument could justify ignoring the clear text of the statute.

Plaintiffs' structural argument incorrectly presupposed that §1182(f) does not authorize the President to revoke Congressional policy judgments. They argued that Travel Ban EO-3 actually countermanded Congressional power and

---

[296] *Id.* (quoting Holder v. Humanitarian Law Project, 561 U.S. 1, 35 (2010)).

[297] *Id.*

[298] *Id.* (citing Hawaii v. Trump, 878 F.3d 662, 688 (2017)).

prerogative because the INA "already specified a two-part solution to aliens seeking entry from countries that do not share sufficient information with the United States."[299] First, Congress implemented an individualized vetting process that placed the burden of proof on the alien to prove his admissibility.[300] Next, instead of banning entry of foreign nationals from particular countries, Congress encouraged information sharing such as through a "Visa Waiver Program" that offered fast-track admission for those countries that cooperated with the United States in this regard.[301] Although the Court agreed that §1182(f) did not authorize the President to expressly override provisions of the INA, the majority still found that the plaintiffs failed to identify any conflict whatsoever between the INA and EO-3 that would prohibit the President from addressing deficiencies that he might identify in the vetting process.[302] To the contrary, the Court easily brushed aside the objections and found that Travel Ban EO-3 supported Congress's individualized approach to the matter, stating:

> The INA sets forth various inadmissibility grounds based on connections to terrorism and criminal history, but those provisions can only work when the consular officer has sufficient (and sufficiently reliable) information to make that determination. The Proclamation [EO-3] promotes the effectiveness of the vetting process by helping to ensure the availability of such information.[303]

In other words, contrary to the plaintiffs' argument, the Court found that Travel Ban EO-3 did not supplant the INA, but instead found that it supplemented the intended purposes of the INA to include the President's participation when he

---

[299]   *Id.* at 2411.

[300]   8 U.S.C. § 1361 (2012).

[301]   *Id.* at § 1187.

[302]   *Trump*, 138 S. Ct. at 2411.

[303]   *Id.*

deemed it was necessary in the interests of the nation to intervene.

Just as the Court found that there was no conflict between Travel Ban EO-3 and the INA's individualized vetting process, it also found that there was no conflict between EO-3 and the Visa Waiver Program.[304] Allowing travel without a visa for short-term visitors, the Visa Waiver Program only applies to those few countries that have entered into a "rigorous security partnership" with the United States.[305] Because Congress had chosen to bestow a special benefit to certain close allies of the United States, did not imply that Congress intended to handcuff the Executive Branch from implementing more severe restrictions against certain aliens or groups of aliens from specific high-risk countries. The Court stated:

> The Visa Waiver Program creates a special exemption for citizens of countries that maintain exemplary security standards and offer "reciprocal [travel] privileges"[306] to United States citizens. But in establishing a select partnership covering less than 20% of the countries in the world, Congress did not address what requirements should govern the entry of countries that fall short of that gold standard— particularly those nations presenting heightened terrorism concerns. Nor did Congress attempt to determine—as the multi-agency review process did—whether those high-risk countries provide a minimum baseline of information to adequately vet their nationals. Once again, this is not a situation

---

[304] 8 U.S.C. § 1187(a)(2)(A) (2012).

[305] Trump v. Hawaii, 138 S. Ct. 2392, 2411 (quoting DEP'T OF HOMELAND SEC., U.S. VISA WAIVER PROGRAM (Apr. 6, 2016), *available at* http://www.dhs.gov/visa-waiver-program).

[306] *Id.* (quoting 8 U.S.C. § 1187(a)(2)(A)).

where "Congress has stepped into the space and solved the exact problem."[307]

Plaintiffs next sought to limit the scope of §1182(f) by looking at the "statutory background and legislative history."[308] Given the clear, plain language of the text, the Court stated there was really no need to consider extra-textual evidence. Ironically, when the Court nevertheless looked at this issue, it found that the plaintiffs' extra-textual evidence actually supported the plain meaning of the statutory provision. Appealing to selective legislative debates about §1182(f), the plaintiffs suggested "the President's suspension power should be limited to exigencies where it would be difficult for Congress to react promptly."[309] For example, during the First and Second World Wars, precursor provisions limited the Executive's exclusion authority to "times of 'war' and 'national emergency.'"[310] Thus, the plaintiffs pointed out that when Congress reenacted §1182(f) in 1952, they borrowed much of the language "nearly verbatim" from the original statute, but left out language pertaining to the national emergency standard. Somehow the plaintiffs believed it logically followed that Congress sought to delegate a "similarly tailored suspension power in the 1952 version of §1182(f)."[311] The Court gave short shift to this historical interpretation and found that the drafting history suggested the exact opposite of what the plaintiffs desired. The Court stated:

> In borrowing "nearly verbatim" from the pre-existing statute, Congress made one critical alteration—it removed the national emergency standard that plaintiffs now seek to reintroduce in

---

[307] *Id.* at 2412 (quoting Tr. of Oral Arg. 53).

[308] *Id.*

[309] *Id.*

[310] *Id.*

[311] *Id.*

another form. Weighing Congress's conscious departure from its wartime statutes against an isolated floor statement, the departure is for more probative. . . . When Congress wishes to condition an exercise of executive authority on the President's finding of an exigency or crisis, it knows how to say just that. . . . Here, Congress instead chose to condition the President's exercise of the suspension of authority on a different finding: that the entry of an alien or class of aliens would be "detrimental to the interests of the United States."[312]

The plaintiffs' final statutory argument was that the President's entry restrictions set out in Travel Ban EO-3 violated the prohibition on discrimination against selected categories so clearly contained §1152(a)(1)(A).[313] Section 1152(a)(1)(A) provides that "no person . . . shall be discriminated against in the issuance of an immigrant visa because of the person's race, sex, nationality, place of birth, or place of residence.[314] Plaintiffs contended that the provision should also be interpreted to prohibit nationality-based discrimination throughout the entire immigration process, to include Travel Ban EO-3.[315] The Court easily rejected that interpretation because "it ignore[d] the basic distinction between admissibility determinations and visa issuance that runs throughout the INA."[316] The Court explained the distinction, stating:

> Section 1182 defines the pool of individuals who are admissible to the United States. Its restrictions come into play at two points in the process of gaining entry (or admission) into the United States. First, any alien who is inadmissible under §1182 (based on, for

---

[312] *Id.* at 2412–13 (citations omitted).

[313] *Id.* at 2413.

[314] *Id.* (quoting 8 U.S.C. § 1152(a)(1)(A) (2012)).

[315] *Id.* at 2413–14.

[316] *Id.* at 2414.

Trump Judges

example, health risks, criminal history, or foreign policy consequences) is screened out as "ineligible to receive a visa." Second, even if a consular officer issues a visa, entry into the United States is not guaranteed. As every visa application explains, a visa does not entitle an alien to enter the United States "if, upon arrival," an immigration officer determines that the applicant is "inadmissible under this chapter, or any other provision of law"— including §1182(f).

* * * *

Sections 1182(f) and 1152(a)(1)(A) thus operate in different spheres: §1182 defines the universe of aliens who are admissible into the United States (and therefore eligible to receive a visa). Once §1182 sets the boundaries of admissibility into the United States, §1152(a)(1)(A) prohibits discrimination in the allocation of immigrant visas based on nationality and other traits. The distinction between admissibility—to which §1152(a)(1)(A) does not apply—and visa issuance—to which it does—is apparent from the text of the provision, which specifies only that its protections apply to the "issuance" of "immigrant visa[s]," without mentioning admissibility or entry. Had Congress instead intended in §1152(a)(1)(A) to constrain the President's power to determine who may enter the country, it could easily have chosen language directed to that end. "The fact that [Congress] did not adopt [a] readily available and apparent alternative strongly supports "the conclusion that §1152(a)(1)(A) does not limit the President's delegated authority under §1182(f).[317]

At the end of the day, the plaintiffs were unable to provide any contradiction with any other provisions in the INA, allowing the Court to, with minimal intellectual effort,

---

[317] *Id.* at 2414–15 (citations omitted).

150

easily conclude that the President did not exceed his delegated authority under §1182(f).[318] In slamming home the fact that Travel Ban EO-3 was clearly within the scope of the Executive's authority under the INA, the majority noted that the four justices that dissented never really focused on attacking Trump's Travel Ban EO-3 on the basis of a statutory argument.

– Muslim Ban and
Living Constitutionalist Dissent –

Fully embraced by living constitutionalist Justice Sotomayor in her poorly reasoned and mean spirited dissent, the plaintiffs' dispositive argument was that Travel Ban EO-3 was issued by President Trump for the sole purpose of excluding Muslims in violation of the First Amendment's Establishment Clause.[319] The Establishment Clause provides that "Congress shall make no law respecting an establishment of religion, or prohibiting the free exercise thereof[.]"[320] As a practical matter, the argument of religious

---

[318] *Id.* at 2415.

[319] *Id.*; *id.* at 2433 (Sotomayer, J., dissenting). Prior courts having found difficulty in resolving cases dealing with the Establishment Clause. *See* Van Orden v. Perry, 545 U.S. 677, 685 (2005) (opinion of Rehnquist, C.J.) (describing inconsistent application of Establishment Clause tests) ("Many of our recent cases simply have not applied [one particular] test. Others have applied it only after concluding that the challenged practice was invalid under a different Establishment Clause test."); *id.* at 692-93 (Thomas, J., concurring) (describing the "inconsistent guideposts [the Court] has adopted for addressing Establishment Clause challenges"); *see also* Smith v. Jefferson Cty. Bd. of School Comm'rs, 788 F.3d 580, 596 (6th Cir. 2015) (Batchelder, C.J., concurring in part) ("For more than four decades, courts have struggled with how to decide Establishment Clause cases, as the governing framework has profoundly changed several times. . . . This confusion has led our court to opine that the judiciary is confined to '*Establishment Clause* purgatory.' ") (quoting ACLU v. Mercer Cty., 432 F.3d 624, 636 (6th Cir. 2005)).

[320] U.S. CONST. amend. I.

discrimination on the part of the President had always been the center of gravity argument for those who opposed all of the Trump travel bans. Setting out her premise, Sotomayor inaccurately summed up the question as follows:

> [T]he dispositive and narrow question here is whether a reasonable observer, presented with all "openly available data," the text and "historical context" of the Proclamation [EO-3], and the "specific sequence of events" leading up to it, would conclude that the primary purpose of the Proclamation [EO-3] is to disfavor Islam and its adherents by excluding them from the country.[321]

Then, having poised the question, Sotomayor was absolutely certain in her response about what her strawman "reasonable observer" must conclude:

> The answer is unquestionably yes. Taking all the relevant evidence together, a reasonable observer would conclude that the Proclamation [EO-3] was driven primarily by anti-Muslim animus, rather than by the Government's asserted national-security justifications.[322]

The Court's majority began by addressing the matter by first considering whether or not the plaintiffs had the requisite standing to bring their Establishment Clause challenge before the Court. This was an issue because the entry restrictions set out by Travel Ban EO-3 did not apply to the plaintiffs directly, but to foreign nationals seeking entry into the United States.

> Federal courts have authority under the Constitution to decide legal question only in the course of resolving "Cases" or "Controversies."[323] One of the essential elements of a legal case or controversy is that the plaintiff have standing to sue. Standing

---

[321] Trump v. Hawaii, 138 S. Ct. at 2438 (Sotomayor, J., dissenting).

[322] *Id.*

[323] *Id.* at 2416 (citing U.S. CONST. art. III, § 2).

requires more than just a "keen interest in the issue."[324] It requires allegations—and, eventually, proof—that the plaintiff "personal[ly]" suffered a concrete and particularized injury in connection with the conduct about which he complains.[325] In a case arising from an alleged violation of the Establishment Clause, a plaintiff must show, as in other cases, that he is "directly affected by the laws and practices against which [his] complaints are directed.[326]

The three individual plaintiffs argued that they had a concrete and particularized injury because Travel Ban EO-3 separated them from certain relatives seeking entry into the United States. This was an issue of common ground between the originalist and the living constitutionalist and the Court agreed with the plaintiffs that a person's desire to be with their relatives is "sufficiently concrete and particularized to form the basis of an Article III injury in fact,"[327] giving the individual plaintiffs the proper standing to challenge the exclusion of their relatives under the Establishment Clause.

– This President vs. The President –

The Court next addressed the matter of the whether Travel Ban EO-3 was issued for an unconstitutional purpose, violating the Establishment Clause by targeting Muslims for unfavorable treatment.[328] Again, the plaintiffs alleged that the true purpose of EO-3 was religious animus, making the national security concerns about vetting and agency review

---

[324] *Id.* (quoting Hollingsworth v. Perry, 570 U.S. 693, 700 (2013)).

[325] *Id.* (citing Spokeo, Inc. v. Robins, 136 S. Ct. 1540 (2016)).

[326] *Id.* (quoting School Dist. of Abington Township v. Schempp, 374 U.S. 203, 224, n.9 (1963)).

[327] *Id.*

[328] Trump v. Hawaii, 138 S. Ct. at 2416–17.

regimens mere pretexts for discriminating against Muslims.[329] Of course, as with all the previous district court challenges, the center of the plaintiffs' argument revolved around the series of offending statements about Muslims made by the President and some of his advisors, statements that the Court took ample note of in its majority opinion.[330] Factually, since Travel Ban EO-3 was facially neutral toward religion, the plaintiffs could only ask the Court to nevertheless "probe the sincerity of the stated justifications"[331] for issuing Travel Ban EO-3 by reference to extrinsic statements, most which were made by candidate Donald Trump, not President Donald Trump.

Indeed, prior to the ruling in *Trump v. Hawaii*, a great many pundits weighed in concerning the baseline issues upon which the Court would ultimately anchor its decision.[332] Perhaps the best prognosis about the Court's thinking came from THE WASHINGTON POST judicial reporter Robert Barnes who said that the Justices would decide the legality of Travel Ban EO-3 under the rubric of "this president," i.e., Donald Trump versus "the president," i.e., the power of the Executive.[333] Given that Congress had delegated sweeping powers to "the president" to bar "the entry of any aliens or of any class of aliens into the United States,"[334] some predicted that the Court might only evaluate

---

[329] *Id.* at 2417.

[330] *See supra* note 239 and accompanying text where the Fourth Circuit recounts anti-Muslim statements.

[331] *Trump*, 138 S. Ct. at 2418.

[332] Rachel Wolfe, *Vox Sentences: The Supreme Court Isn't About to Join the #Resistance*, VOX (Apr. 25, 2018, 8:00 PM), https://www.vox.com/vox-sentences/2018/4/25/17282436/vox-sentences-supreme-court-travel-ban.

[333] David French, *Will the Supreme Court Join the #Resistance?*, NAT'L REV. (Apr. 24, 2018 2:39 PM), https://www.nationalreview.com/2018/04/donald-trump-travel-ban-supreme-court-resistance/.

[334] 8 U.S.C. § 1182(f) ("Whenever the President finds that the entry of any aliens or of any class of aliens into the United States would be detrimental to the interests of the United States, he may by proclamation,

the legality of Travel Ban EO-3 on the basis of the words in the order and nothing else. Under such a review, Travel Ban EO-3 would surely stand. On the other hand, if the Court felt that the words of "this president," President Trump, spoken outside the four corners of the order were so egregious, it might depart from settled precedent such as *Kleindienst v. Mandel*,[335] and "create new precedent specifically designed to rein him [Donald Trump] in."[336] As it turned out, the "Barnes approach" was exactly what the Court did, although as will be detailed below, the Court employed a standard of review set at the lowest level of judicial scrutiny.[337]

So, while the plaintiffs argued that the Trump statements provided clear evidence of an Establishment Clause violation—one religious denomination was preferred over another—the Court rightly assessed the question by weighing the President's words against the President's authority.[338] Despite vociferous lamentations of dissenting justices Sotomayor and Ginsburg, the Court would consider the cited language of President Trump as a far less persuasive matter.[339] To be sure, there can be no question that a great many of President Trump's words not only ran contrary to fundamental standards of respect and tolerance, but some of them constituted an alarming assault on the

---

and for such period as he shall deem necessary, suspend the entry of all aliens or any class of aliens as immigrants or nonimmigrants, or impose on the entry of aliens any restrictions he may deem to be appropriate.").

[335] Kleindienst v. Mandel, 408 U.S. 753 (1972), *aff'd*, 137 S. Ct. 2080, 2086 (2017), *aff'd*, 138 U.S. 2392, 2416 (2018).

[336] *See generally* Kleindienst v. Mandel, 408 U.S. 753 (1972), *aff'd*, 137 S. Ct. 2080, 2086 (2017), *aff'd*, 138 U.S. 2392, 2416 (2018); *see also* French, *supra* note 343.

[337] *Trump*, 138 S. Ct. at 2420.

[338] *Id.* at 2416–17 (quoting Larson v. Valente, 456 U.S. 228, 244 (1982) ("[T]he clearest command of the Establishment Clause is that one religious denomination cannot be preferred over another.").

[339] *Id.* at 2417–18.

cherished American liberty of religious freedom.[340]   Still, given that Travel Ban EO-3 had no hint of a "religious" test within the four corners of the order, the majority refocused the matter of the legality of EO-3 back to the weightier side of the equation—"the president"—stating the following:

> [It is] the significance of those [offensive] statements in reviewing a Presidential directive, neutral on its face, addressing a matter within the core of executive responsibility. In doing so we must consider not only the statements of a *particular President*, but also the authority of the *Presidency* itself [emphasis added].[341]

Before addressing the "statements of a particular President"—the "this President" side of the coin—the Court once again reiterated the "authority of the Presidency"—the "the President"—side of the coin. The Court took firm note of the fact that for more than a century it has been the constant juridical position that the entry of foreign nationals is a question better suited for the Legislature or the Executive, not the Courts.[342] Without a doubt, the majority correctly understood that the Constitution did not task it to second guess a sitting President as long as the reasons for his actions were "facially legitimate and bona fide."[343]

---

[340]   *See* Ben Jacobs, *Donald Trump's Plan to Bar Muslims May Be an Outlandish Policy Too Far*, THE GUARDIAN (Dec. 8, 2015, 1:39 PM), https://www.theguardian.com/us-news/2015/dec/08/donald-trumps-plan-to-bar-muslims-may-be-an-outlandish-policy-too-far (" 'Well, I think this whole notion that somehow we need to say no more Muslims and just ban a whole religion goes against everything we stand for and believe in,' responded former US vice-president Dick Cheney in a radio interview. 'I mean, religious freedom's been an important part of our, our history.' ").

[341]   *Trump*, 138 S. Ct. at 2418.

[342]   *Id.* Still, while foreign nationals seeking entry into the United States have no right to admission in the Constitution, the Court "has engaged in . . . judicial inquiry when the denial of a visa allegedly burdens the constitutional rights of a U.S. citizen." *Id.* at 2402.

[343]   *Id.* at 2419.

Accordingly, as would be the case for an originalist justice, the Court simply followed established precedent as set out in a variety of cases to include *Kleindienst v. Mandel*,[344] which was specifically cited with strong approval.

In *Mandel*, the Court rejected claims that the government was required to grant entry into the United States to a self-described Marxist journalist from Belgium who had been invited to speak at an academic conference at Stanford University in California.[345] The plaintiffs, a collection of

---

[344] Kleindienst v. Mandel, 408 U.S. 753 (1972).

[345] Under the law as it then existed, entry into the United States was banned to individuals who advocated or published "the economic, international, and governmental doctrines of world communism."

(a) Except as otherwise provided in this Act, the following classes of aliens shall be ineligible to receive visas and shall be excluded from admission into the United States:

* * * *

(28) Aliens who are, or at any time have been, members of any of the following classes:

* * * *

(D) Aliens . . . who advocate [or who are members of or affiliated with any organization that advocates] the economic, international, and governmental doctrines of world communism or the establishment in the United States of a totalitarian dictatorship. . . .

* * * *

(G) Aliens who write or publish, or cause to be written or published, or who knowingly circulate, distribute, print, or display, or knowingly cause to be circulated, distributed, printed, published, or displayed, or who knowingly have in their possession for the purpose of circulation, publication, distribution, or display, any written or printed matter, advocating or teaching opposition to all organized government, or advocating or teaching . . . (v) the economic, international, and governmental doctrines of world communism or the establishment in the United States of a totalitarian dictatorship.

8 U.S.C. § 1182 (1972) *amended* Immigration Act of 1990, Pub. L. No. 101-649, 104 STAT. 4978. (leaving only Section 1182(a)(3)(D) "IMMIGRANT MEMBERSHIP IN TOTALITARIAN PARTY. (i) IN GENERAL. Any immigrant who is or has been a member of or affiliated

scholars and professors, argued that their First Amendment right to "receive information"[346] from Mr. Ernest Mandel was implicated. Although the Court in *Mandel* agreed that the First Amendment was most certainly implicated by banning Mandel from the country, the Court's majority strictly limited its review to whether the Executive gave a "facially legitimate and bona fide" reason for the exclusion of the self-proclaimed Marxist.[347] Given the broad authority wielded by the political branches over restricting entry into the United States, the *Mandel* Court upheld Mandel's exclusion stating:

> [W]hen the Executive exercises this [delegated] power negatively on the basis of a facially legitimate and bona fide reason, the courts will neither look behind the exercise of that discretion, nor test it by balancing its justification against the First Amendment interests of those who seek personal communication with the applicant [emphasis added].[348]

In applying this very paragraph set out in *Mandel* to the President's delegated power set out in Travel Ban EO-3, the Court added that it would not test the Executive's power "against the asserted constitutional interests of U.S. citizens."[349] In her dissent, Justice Sotomayor suggested that *Mandel* did not apply to Travel Ban EO-3, but the majority unequivocally disagreed and found that *Mandel's* standard of review "has particular force" in entry and immigration cases when they overlap with "the area of national security."[350] Indeed, the Court held that a conventional

---

with the Communist or any other totalitarian party (or subdivision or affiliate thereof), domestic or foreign, is inadmissible.").

[346] *Mandel*, 408 U.S. at 764–765.

[347] *Id.* at 770.

[348] *Id.*

[349] Trump v. Hawaii, 138 S. Ct. 2392, 2419 (2018).

[350] *Id.*; *see also id.* at 2440–41 (Sotomayor J., dissenting).

application of *Mandel*, which asks only whether the "policy is facially legitimate and bona fide," would most certainly put an end to any further judicial review and completely uphold the validity of Travel Ban EO-3. Curiously, however, the Government suggested in oral arguments before the Court that it might be "appropriate here for the [Court's] inquiry to extend beyond the facially neutrality of the order [EO-3]."[351] Thus, with the government unilaterally opening the proverbial Pandora box, and perhaps for the Court's stated purposes of engaging in a full review on the merits, the majority decided that it "may look behind the face of the Proclamation [EO-3] to the extent of applying rational basis review."[352]

Set at an admittedly low level of judicial scrutiny, the rational basis standard considers whether the entry policy set out in Travel Ban EO-3 is reasonably related to the government's stated objective to protect the country and improve vetting deficiencies. As a result, the Court could consider extrinsic evidence outside the language of EO-3—such as candidate Trump's cited words—but they would still uphold the travel ban so long as "it can reasonably be understood to result from a justification independent of unconstitutional grounds,"[353] such as serving national security interests. In its review, the Court noted that while the dissent placed great importance on the fact "that five of the seven nations currently included in the Proclamation [EO-3] have Muslim-majority populations,"[354] the majority pointed out that this fact alone fails to infer religious hostility. To the contrary, particularly telling for the Court was the fact that Travel Ban EO-3 only covered 8% of the world's Muslim population and was limited to countries

---

[351]   *Id.*

[352]   *Id.*

[353]   *Id.*

[354]   *Id.* at 2421.

previously designated by the Obama Administration as a risk to national security.

The Court also provided three additional features in support of the fact that the entry policy served a legitimate national security interest and weighed against the contention that Travel Ban EO-3 was motivated by anti-Muslim animus. First, since the policy had been introduced, three Muslim-majority countries—Iraq, Sudan, and Chad—had been removed from the list. Second, for those countries still subject to entry restrictions, Travel Ban EO-3 provided exceptions for various foreign nationals in those Muslim nations. Finally, EO-3 included an internal waiver program "open to all covered foreign nationals seeking entry as immigrants or nonimmigrants."[355]

Entirely appropriate, the majority specifically took time to respond to Justice Sotomayor's dissenting opinion where she drew a ridiculously unwarranted parallel between the World War II era case of *Korematsu v. United States* and the majority's decision in *Trump v. Hawaii*.[356] Agreeing with the majority in their formal repudiation of *Korematsu*, Sotomayor nevertheless openly accused the majority of "blindly accepting the Government's misguided invitation to sanction a discriminatory policy motivated by animosity toward a disfavored group, all in the name of a superficial claim of national security[.]"[357] The majority clearly took offense at this unfair accusation that they were engaging in racist wrongdoing and stated:

---

[355] *Id.*

[356] *Id.* at 2423; Korematsu v. U.S., 323 U.S. 214 (1944) *abrogated by* Trump v. Hawaii, 138 S. Ct. 2392 (2018). *See Trump*, 138 S. Ct. at 2447.

[357] *See Trump*, 138 S. Ct. at 2448 ("By blindly accepting the Government's misguided invitation to sanction a discriminatory policy motivated by animosity toward a disfavored group, all in the name of a superficial claim of national security, the Court redeploys the same dangerous logic underlying *Korematsu* and merely replaces one "gravely wrong" decision with another.") (Sotomayor J., dissenting).

Whatever rhetorical advantage the dissent [Sotomayor] may see in doing so, *Korematsu* has nothing to do with this case. The forcible relocation of U.S. citizens to concentration camps, solely and explicitly on the basis of race, is objectively unlawful and outside the scope of Presidential authority. But it is wholly inapt to liken that morally repugnant order to a facially neutral policy denying certain foreign nationals the privilege of admission.[358]

Trump v. Hawaii was decided correctly. When measured against both the statutory and inherent power of the Executive in restricting the entry of aliens into the United States, President Trump's remarks leading up to the order received little script by the Court. The majority had no stomach to second guess a sitting President particularly having established that the reasons for Travel Ban EO-3 were "facially legitimate and bona fide[.]"[359] Thus, the Court rightly found that: "The Proclamation is expressly premised on legitimate purposes: preventing entry of nationals who cannot be adequately vetted and inducing other nations to improve their practices. The text says nothing about religion."[360]

Although the Court made no judgement on the policy considerations behind Travel Ban EO-3, it specifically found no evidence on the face of Travel Ban EO-3 that demonstrated the discriminatory bias that opponents so loudly proclaimed. The text of Travel Ban EO-3 was neutral, a strong argument that EO-3 was not a function of religious discrimination but of national security. Coupled with the fact that the vast majority of Muslim-majority nations were never the focus of any of the three travel bans, is the incontrovertible fact that the nations that were targeted were deeply associated with the continuing threat of radical

---

[358] *Id.* at 2423.

[359] Trump v. Hawaii, 138 S. Ct. 2392, 2420 (2018).

[360] *Id.* at 2421.

Islamic terrorism. Again, Travel Ban EO-3 was not based on the nationality of the individual or Muslim animus, but on the fact that certain named governments had not provided the necessary guarantees about the state of their security and vetting procedures.

In terms of upholding the rule of law, the originalist justices on the Court certainly got it right in *Trump vs. Hawaii*, but there is no doubt that the various off hand negative remarks about Muslims made by President Trump cast an unnecessary shadow over one of the most sacred pillars of our republic—religious freedom. While the tides of jurisprudential history rise and fall, it is vitally important that religious tolerance must not wash up on the shoreline. Justice Kennedy understood the greater picture in this regard. Given that Justice Kennedy knew when he penned his concurrence with the majority that this would be his last case as a Supreme Court justice, it is no surprise that much of his short three-paragraph opinion exhibited a compelling poeticism about the necessity of religious tolerance regardless of ideological inclinations or political advantage.[361] The nation rightfully expects our leaders to avoid even the slightest appearance of evil when it comes to freedom of religion and religious tolerance. Kennedy wrote words of great wisdom:

> The First Amendment prohibits the establishment of religion and promises the free exercise of religion. From these safeguards, and from the guarantee of freedom of speech, it follows there is freedom of belief and expression. It is an urgent necessity that officials adhere to these constitutional guarantees and mandates in all their actions, even in the sphere of foreign affairs. An anxious world must know that our Government remains committed always to the

---

[361] *See* Tessa Berenson, *What Does the Supreme Court's Ruling on the Travel Ban Really Say?*, TIMES (July 8, 2018), http://time.com/5324727/whats-hidden-inside-the-supreme-courts-ruling-on-the-travel-ban/ (suggesting that Justice Kennedy's concluding paragraph was seeking an "epitaph for his career on the bench[.]").

liberties the Constitution seeks to preserve and protect, so that freedom extends outward, and lasts.[362]

---

[362] *Trump*, 138 S. Ct. at 2424.

Chapter Seven
Trump Bias in the Courts

"I can't imagine what this place would be—
I can't imagine what the country would be with
Donald Trump as our president. For the country, it could
be four years. For the court, it could be—
I don't even want to contemplate that."[363]

– Ruth Bader Ginsburg

Progressives understand completely that no single American has done more to thwart their agenda to destroy the establishment pillars than Donald J. Trump. Accordingly, in their minds, Trump must be resisted at every turn to include impeachment—even if no crimes can be cited in the articles of impeachment! Proof of this is abundant to include the absolutely farcical partisan Democrat impeachment of President Trump which ended in February 2020 with his acquittal. One thing is clear, there can be no serious debate regarding the existence of an extreme anti-Trump animus residing in the progressive wing of the Democrat party.

In turn, much has been written about the existence of a "deep state" apparatus of progressives operating within the Executive Branch and devoted to obstructing the agenda of the Trump Administration.[364] With such an atmosphere of

---

[363] Adam Liptak, *Ruth Bader Ginsburg, No Fan of Donald Trump, Critiques Latest Term*, N.Y. TIMES (July 10, 2016), https://www. nytimes.com/2016/07/11/us/politics/ruth-bader-ginsburg-no-fan-of-donald-trump-critiques-latest-term.html.

[364] *See* Julie H. Davis, *'Deep State'? Until Now, It Was a Foreign Concept*, Mar. 6, 2017 at A19 ("Neither Mr. Trump nor Mr. Bannon has used the term "deep state" publicly. But each has argued that there is an

distrust and animosity at work, it is not unreasonable to wonder if some of the lower federal court decisions and perhaps even the Sotomayor/Ginsburg dissent in *Trump vs. Hawaii* might, to some degree, be tainted by an emotional "anti-Trump animus."[365]

Indeed, in light of the well settled case law surrounding the validity of Travel Ban EO-3, such as *Mandel*,[366] *Fiallo*,[367] and *Din*[368] many see only a political motivation by certain federal judges to harm President Trump. For instance, in his forceful dissent objecting to the Fourth Circuit's upholding of the nationwide injunction of the travel ban, federal circuit judge Paul Niemeyer alleged that the majority was motivated in their ruling not by the law but by "political" animus against President Trump:

> In looking behind the face of the government's action for facts to show the allege bad faith, rather than looking for bad faith on the face of the executive action itself, the majority grants itself the power to conduct an extratextual search for evidence suggesting bad faith, which is exactly what three

orchestrated effort underway, fueled by leaks and enabled by the news media, to cut down the new president and interfere with his agenda").

[365] *See* David French, *Will the Supreme Court Join the #Resistance?*, NAT'L REV. (April 24, 2018, 2:39 PM), https://www.nationalreview.com /2018/04/donald-trump-travel-ban-supreme-court-resistance/ (questioning the political motivations of some members of the Supreme Court).

[366] Kleindienst v. Mandel, 408 U.S. 753 (1972).

[367] *See* Fiallo v. Bell, 430 U.S. 787, 799–800 (1977) (holding (the Immigration and Nationality Act of 1952 are not unconstitutional by virtue of the exclusion of the relationship between an illegitimate child and his natural father from the preferences accorded by the Act to the "child" or "parent" of a United States citizen or lawful permanent resident.").

[368] *See* Kerry v. Din, 135 S. Ct. 2128 (2015) (concluding that Din received all the process to which she was entitled finding the most substantial instruction in the Court's decision in Kleindienst v. Mandel, 408 U.S. 753 (1972)).

Supreme Court opinions have prohibited. *Mandel,
Fiallo,* and *Din* have for decades been entirely clear
that courts are not free to look behind these sorts of
exercises of executive discretion in search of
circumstantial evidence of alleged bad faith. The
majority, now for the first time, rejects these holdings
in favor of its *politically desired* outcome [emphasis
added].[369]

Without question, it is hard to imagine a more
problematic situation for the country than an unbridled
federal judiciary overreaching and micro-managing issues
regarding national security—substituting their judgment for
the President's based on political motivations.[370] Of course,

---

[369] Int'l Refugee Assistance Project v. Trump, 857 F.3d 554, 648 (4th
Cir. 2017) (Neimeyer, J., Dissenting), *vacated as moot,* 138 S. Ct. 353
(2017).

[370] Dissenting Justice Antonio Scalia often warned of the harm to
America's constitutional fabric when the judicial branch overreaches
into the realm of the executive branch. *See generally* Boumediene v.
Bush 128 S. Ct. 2229 (2008) (SCALIA J., Dissenting).

And if the understood scope of the writ of habeas corpus was
"designed to restrain" (as the Court says) the actions of the
Executive, the understood limits upon that scope were (as the
Court seems not to grasp) just as much "designed to restrain"
the incursions of the Third Branch. "Manipulation" of the
territorial reach of the writ by the Judiciary poses just as much
a threat to the proper separation of powers as "manipulation"
by the Executive. As I will show below, manipulation is what
is afoot here. The understood limits upon the writ deny our
jurisdiction over the habeas petitions brought by these enemy
aliens, and entrust the President with the crucial wartime
determinations about their status and continued confinement.

* * * *

But so long as there are some places to which habeas does not
run—so long as the Court's new "functional" test will not be
satisfied in every case—then there will be circumstances in
which "it would be possible for the political branches to govern
without legal constraint." Or, to put it more impartially, areas
in which the legal determinations of the other branches will be
(shudder!) supreme. In other words, judicial supremacy is not
really assured by the constitutional rule that the Court creates.

whether in the majority or in the dissent, all justices will assert with straight faces that their legal opinions are rendered solely as a consequence of following the law, not politics. Still, one cannot wonder if the "law they follow" might not sometimes be dictated by their positions set along an ideological spectrum, which as outlined previously in this book ranges from the originalist view of the Constitution to the living constitutionalist view of the Constitution.[371]

For example, one point of interest in the *Trump v. Hawaii* dissent of Justice Sotomayor, with whom Justice Ginsburg joined, is that there seems to be no consideration whatsoever to the possibility that President Trump's anti-Muslim statements, predominately made on the campaign trail, might *not reflect* what he really believes, particularly when viewed against the actual language contained in Travel Ban EO-3.[372] They are simply biased against President Trump.

> The gap between rationale and rule leads me to conclude that the Court's ultimate, unexpressed goal is to preserve the power to review the confinement of enemy prisoners held by the Executive anywhere in the world. The "functional" test usefully evades the precedential landmine of *Eisentrager* but is so inherently subjective that it clears a wide path for the Court to traverse in the years to come.

Id. at 833–34, 843.

[371] *See* Eric Segall, *The Supreme Court is About to Get a Lot Less Honest About its Fake Originalism*, SLATE (July 16, 2018, 1:45 PM), https://slate.com/news-and-politics/2018/07/the-supreme-court-is-about-to-get-less-honest-about-fake-originalism.html. ("[Justice Kennedy] will be sorely missed because, although all the justices decide cases based on their own modern sensibilities, Kennedy was one of the few, left or right, to openly admit it."); *but see* Mark W. Hendrickson, *The U.S. Constitution: Living, Breathing Document or Dead Letter?*, VISION AND VALUES (May 28, 2009), http://www.visionandvalues.org/2009/05/the-us-constitution-living-breathing-document-or-dead-letter/ ("Liberals and progressives believe that the Constitution is a living, breathing document that should evolve with the times. They want Supreme Court justices to be flexible in interpreting the Constitution and adapting 18th-century language to 21st-century applications.").

[372] Trump v. Hawaii, 138 S. Ct. 2392, 2433–40 (2018) (Sotomayor, J., dissenting). *See also* Veronica Rocha, et al., *President Trump Meets Kim*

In his concurring opinion, originalist Justice Clarence Thomas certainly found this to be the case stating succinctly that "even on its own terms, the plaintiffs' proffered evidence of [President Trump's] anti-Muslim discrimination is unpersuasive."[373] In other words, Thomas was not willing to take a handful of "cherry picked" offensive statements to then paint President Trump as a "racist" and all things that he subsequently undertook in terms of his travel ban to be irrevocably tainted by racism. Employing common sense, the consummate originalist seemed to easily understand what Sotomayor disingenuously rejected out of hand—it is not uncommon for prominent government figures, to include President Trump, to utter offensive remarks that might not necessarily reveal what that person actually believes as intrinsic truth.

Without question, one of the occupational hazards of anyone who engages in public speaking is the occasional misstatement, wrong statement, or even stupid statement. This phenomenon reaches across the political aisle. For instance, former Vice President Joe Biden is infamous in this regard with one of his most bizarre gaffs taking place at a speech he gave to the Institute for Advanced Learning and Research in Danville, Virginia, where he told a largely black audience that Republicans desired to "put y'all back in

---

Jong Un, CNN (June 12, 2018, 11:03 AM), https://www.cnn.com/politics/live-news/trump-kim-jong-un-meeting-summit/h_97ccc50308b 493e9f22e108ef7402249 ("I may be wrong and stand before you in six months and say, 'Hey I was wrong,' before pausing. 'I don't think I'll ever admit that,' he said.") (internal quotations removed); Karen Tumulty, *Trump: Never Wrong, Never Sorry, Never Responsible*, WASH. POST (Sept. 16, 2016), https://www.washingtonpost.com/politics/trump-never-wrong-never-sorry-never-responsible/2016/09/16/88446d0e-7c1c-11e6-ac8e-cf8e0dd91dc7_story.html?noredirect=on&utm_term=.1f63 d89dc02f (" 'I fully think apologizing is a great thing, but you have to be wrong,' Trump told 'Tonight Show' host Jimmy Fallon a year ago. 'I will absolutely apologize sometime in the distant future if I'm ever wrong.' ").

[373] *Trump*, 138 S. Ct. at 2424 (Thomas J., concurring).

chains."[374]   Surely, no one really believes that Joe Biden advocates such nonsense.

Even Justice Sotomayor herself has made extremely offensive public statements regarding what some might easily construe as racist and/or extreme bias against white males.[375] For instance, it is widely reported that Sotomayor remarked:

> Whether born from experience or inherent physiological or cultural differences . . . our gender and national origins may and will make a difference in our judging. Justice O'Connor has often been cited as saying that a wise old man and wise old woman will reach the same conclusion in deciding cases. . . . I am . . . not so sure that I agree with the statement. First, as Professor Martha Minnow has noted, there can never be a universal definition of wise. Second, I would hope that *a wise Latina woman with the richness of her experiences would more often than not reach a better conclusion than a*

[374]   Ashley Killough, *Biden: Romney's Wall Street Will 'Put Y'all Back in Chains'*, CNN (Aug. 14, 2012, 12:24 PM), http://politicalticker. blogs.cnn.com/2012/08/14/biden-romneys-wall-street-will-put-yall-back-in-chains/; James Nye, *'They're Going to Put Y'all Back in Chains' Says Joe Biden to Black Crowd about Romney and Ryan Ticket*, ORIGINAL PEOPLE (Aug. 14, 2012, 3:33 PM), http://originalpeople. org/theyre-going-to-put-yall-back-in-chains-says-joe-biden-to-black-crowd-about-romney-and-ryan-ticket/ ("where a majority of people are African American.").

[375]   Charlie Savage, *A Judge's View of Judging Is on the Record*, N.Y. TIMES (May 14, 2009), https://www.nytimes.com/2009/05/15/us/15judge.html (referring to when she said "I would hope that a wise Latina woman with the richness of her experiences would more often than not reach a better conclusion than a white male who hasn't lived that life."); Frank James, *Sotomayor's 'Wise Latina' Line Maybe Not So Wise*, NPR (May 27, 2009), https://www.npr.org/sections/thetwo-way/2009/05/sotomayors_wise_latina_line_ma.html.

white male who hasn't lived that life [emphasis added].[376]

Just as President Trump has denied allegations that he holds any religious animus against Muslims, Sotomayor has similarly denied charges of racism against white males.[377] Yet, Sotomayor was not willing to even remotely entertain the idea that President Trump might not hold discriminatory views about Muslims, despite his inappropriate statements. It is certain, however, that she would demand that all "forgive" her remarks.

The possibility that President Trump does not hold discriminatory views of Muslims, as Justice Thomas correctly understands, only requires one to examine more closely the unorthodox speaking style of President Trump. Even the most vociferous critics of President Trump have to admit (although they never will) that Trump's use of bombastic rhetoric and bluster as a negotiating strategy can produce positive results.[378] One need only consider that his yearlong hard line against the Communist regime of North Korea which consisted of economic sanctions, military saber waving, and mocking Trump taunts to Kim Jong-un—"Little Rocket Man"—brought the dictator to the negotiating table

---

[376] *Id.* ("Still, Judge Sotomayor questioned whether achieving impartiality "is possible in all, or even, in most, cases." She added, "And I wonder whether by ignoring our differences as women or men of color we do a disservice both to the law and society.").

[377] *See* Saagar Enjeti, *Trump Denies Hating Muslims: 'I Feel Love For All People'*, THE DAILY CALLER (Jan. 29, 2018, 12:30 PM), http://dailycaller.com/2018/01/29/trump-denies-hating-muslims-i-feel-love-for-all-people/. ("President Donald Trump denied feeling animus towards Muslims during a wide-ranging interview with British TV personality Piers Morgan.").

[378] *See* David Jackson & Michael Collins, *Trump Celebrates 'Historic' Trade Deal with Canada and Mexico, but Hard Work Isn't Over*, USA TODAY (Oct. 3, 2018), https://www.usatoday.com/story/news/politics/2018/10/01/nafta-despite-new-trade-deal-hard-work-isnt-over/1489998 002/ (describing the Trump Administration's new USAMCA economic treaty).

regarding nuclear disarmament.[379] The White House said that the "campaign of maximum pressure" had created the "appropriate atmosphere for dialogue with North Korea," but the language and tone of President Trump were certainly contributing factors.[380]

While his political opponents consistently decry Trump's occasional abandonment of "politically correct" language, one prominent opinion pollster suggests that it is a tenacious argument to view President Trump's language as a precise window into his actual thinking on any given matter.[381] Based on polling data, pollster Lee Carter believes

---

[379] *See* Mark Lander, *Trump Imposes More Sanctions on Pyongyang*, N.Y. TIMES (Feb. 23, 2018), https://www.nytimes.com/2018/02/23/us/politics/trump-north-korea-sanctions.html (announcing new economic sanctions against North Korea and alluding to a "phase 2" which could include military action should the sanctions not work); Donald J. Trump (@realDonaldTrump), TWITTER (Sept. 17, 2017, 4:53 AM), https://twitter.com/realDonaldTrump/status/909384837018112000 ("I spoke with President Moon of South Korea last night. Asked him how Rocket Man is doing. Long gas lines forming in North Korea. Too bad!"); Choe Sang-Hun, *Kim Jung-un Says He Wants Denuclearization in Trump's Current Term,* N.Y. TIMES (Sept. 6, 2018), https://www.nytimes.com/2018/09/06/world/asia/kim-jong-un-donald-trump-denuclearize.html ("Offering an olive branch to President Trump, Kim Jong-un told a South Korean envoy that he wanted to denuclearize North Korea before Mr. Trump's current term ends in early 2021, the envoy said on Thursday."); Donald J. Trump (@realDonaldTrump), TWITTER (Sept. 6, 2018, 3:58 AM), https://twitter.com/realdonaldtrump/status/1037656324010663937?lang=en ("Kim Jong Un of North Korea proclaims 'unwavering faith in President Trump.' Thank you to Chairman Kim. We will get it done together!").

[380] John Lyons, Jeremy Page, & Chun Han Wong, *North Korean Leader Meets with Xi in Surprise China Visit*, THE WALL STREET J. (Mar. 18, 2018), https://www.wsj.com/articles/china-says-north-korean-leader-kim-jong-un-visited-beijing-1522195885.

[381] *FOX & Friends* (FOX television broadcast Sept. 8, 2018) (summing up President Trumps speaking style Lee Carter said "A lot of people have gotten to the point now where they are not taking the President quite so literally [in his political campaign remarks] as a lot of people on the left have taken everything so literally . . . people on the left scratch their

---

that most Americans have now adjusted to the speaking style and temperament of President Trump—particularly when he takes to pontificating with off-hand remarks—and have learned not to take President Trump's words so literally.[382] In this light, in many instances the key to understanding the real meaning of a Trump pronouncement is to listen to him with "the eye rather than the ear." In other words, rather than fixating on individual words to then discern a precise meaning as to future actions, it is far more efficacious to look at the resulting actions to then understand what he "really" meant.

– Loose Lips Sink Ships –

Again, it is undeniable that a great many public figures have made improper and/or offensive statements that can easily be taken out of context by their critics to "prove a point" or simply to "score a point." Just as Presidents don't always speak in a manner considered to be "presidential"— a common criticism of the flamboyant Donald Trump[383]—

---

heads and [do] not understand it [that Trump is not to be taken so literally in his rhetoric].").

[382] *Id.*

[383] *See* Bastien Inzaurralde, *This Linguist Studied the Way Trump Speaks for Two Years. Here's What She Found.*, WASH. POST (July 7, 2017) https://www.washingtonpost.com/news/the-fix/wp/2017/07/07/this-linguist-studied-the-way-trump-speaks-for-two-years-heres-what-she-found/?noredirect=on&utm_term=.d39b92a633de. ("Trump is a "unique" politician because he doesn't speak like one, according to Jennifer Sclafani, an associate teaching professor in Georgetown University's Department of Linguistics."); Charles M. Blow, *Degradation of the Language*, N.Y. TIMES (Apr. 30, 2017), https://www.nytimes.com/2017/05/01/opinion/donald-trump-degradation-of-the-language.html.

America is suffering under the tyranny of gibberish spouted by the lord of his faithful 46 percent. As researchers at Carnegie Mellon pointed out last spring, presidential candidates in general use "words and grammar typical of students in grades 6–8, though Donald Trump tends to lag behind the others." Indeed, among the presidents in the university's analysis,

Supreme Court justices don't always speak in a manner befitting the high station of the neutral judge sitting on the bench of justice. For instance, in the summer of 2016 Justice Ginsburg made a series of very questionable public statements that reflected an extreme anti-Trump bias against then candidate Donald Trump.[384] Realizing that her remarks were at least highly inappropriate and at most could be construed as disqualifying her from ruling on cases involving actions taken by a Trump Administration, Ginsburg quickly issued an apology for calling Trump a "faker" and other derogatory names during 2016 CNN interviews.

> Interview July 7, 2016 with Associated Press: Asked what if Trump won the presidency, Ginsburg said: "I don't want to think about that possibility, but if it should be, then everything is up for grabs."; Interview July 8, 2016 with New York Times: "I can't imagine what this place would be—I can't imagine what the country would be—with Donald Trump as our president. For the country, it could be four years. For the court, it could be—I don't even want to contemplate that. Referring to something she thought her late husband, tax lawyer Martin Ginsburg, would have said, she said: "Now it's time for us to move to New Zealand."; Interview July 11, 2016 with CNN: "He is a faker. He has no consistency about him. He says whatever comes into his head at the moment. He really has an ego. . . . How has he gotten away with not turning over his tax returns? The press seems to be very gentle with him on that. . . . "At first I thought it was funny," she said of Trump's early candidacy. "To think that there's a

---

Trump's vocabulary usage was the lowest and his grammatical usage was only better than one president: George W. Bush.

[384] *See* Tom Kertscher, *What Ruth Bader Ginsburg said About Donald Trump*, POLITIFACT (July 13, 2016, 2:36 PM), https://www.politifact.com/wisconsin/article/2016/jul/13/what-ruth-bader-ginsburg-said-about-donald-trump/.

possibility that he could be president. . . . Update: On July 14, 2016, Ginsburg apologized for her remarks, saying they were "ill-advised."[385]

One of the themes of the acrimonious 2018 Kavanagh Senate hearings was that a judge should cherish and exhibit "common sense"[386] not political bias. In his opening remarks to the Senate committee Kavanagh said: "In deciding cases, a judge must always keep in mind what Alexander Hamilton said in Federalist 83: 'the rules of legal interpretation are rules of common sense.' "[387] In this light, there is no greater source of wisdom when it comes to addressing temptations to hyperventilate over untoward conversation than the words found in the Biblical book of Ecclesiastes. Recognizing that all people commit sins of the tongue, King Solomon cautioned:

> Indeed, there is not a righteous man on earth who continually does good and who never sins. Also, do not take seriously all words which are spoken, so that you will not hear your servant cursing you. For you also have realized that you likewise have many times cursed others.[388]

---

[385] Stephen Francis Ward, *Supreme ICON*, ABA JOURNAL, Oct. 2018, at 37 (Justice Ginsburg's remarks inspired an "I Dissent" Ginsburg pin that was sold to retain chains "Hot Topic, Urban Outfitters and Claire's Accessories . . . as a way to deal with concern about Trump becoming the country's president." *Id.*

[386] *'I will do equal right to the poor and the rich': Brett Kavanaugh's Remarks to the Senate Committee*, USA TODAY (Sept. 4, 2018, 7:07 PM), https://www.usatoday.com/story/news/politics/2018/09/04/brett-kavanaugh-supreme-court-nominees-remarks-senate-committee/1196833002/. ("In deciding cases, a judge must always keep in mind what Alexander Hamilton said in Federalist 83: 'the rules of legal interpretation are rules of common sense.'").

[387] *Id.*

[388] Eccl. 7:20–22 (New American Standard Version) (emphasis added).

Conclusion

*"No free government can stand without virtue in the
people, and a lofty spirit of patriotism."*[389]

– Andrew Jackson

As never before in its history, the very core legal and
moral principles that have sustained Americanism for almost
250 years are under a relentless attack by a coalition of
progressives, socialists, leftists, and their like-minded allies.
Their collective goal is to drastically alter the establishment
pillars upon which this nation was erected and upon which it
has weathered many storms.

Until the election of Donald J. Trump, few conservatives
seemed willing or even able to take on progressive ideology
in a head-to-head fight, particularly when it came to
understanding the absolute necessity of getting more
originalist judges in the federal courts in order to blunt
progressive attacks on America's establishment pillars:
(individual/privacy; marriage; family; and nationalism).
Indeed, given the tremendous power of the Supreme Court
to make law, this goal alone—to appoint originalist judges—
should rank as the key ingredient to the support of any
political leader who seeks the office of president of the
United States of America. To his great credit, President
Trump both realized the threat to American establishment
values and the absolute imperative of appointing originalist
judges—courageous men and women who would blunt and
turn back the forces of progressive ideology.

On the opposite spectrum, Justice Ginsburg and
company recognized the same thing when they dreaded the

---

[389] Andrew Jackson, President of the United States, Farewell Address
(1837), https://liberalarts.utexas.edu/coretexts/_files/resources/texts/
1837%20Jackson%20Farewell%20Address.pdf.

real possibility in 2016 of a Trump presidency. Progressives salivated at the thought of Hillary Clinton winning the election because it meant that they would have the power to stack the federal courts with living constitutionalists and accelerate the demise of Americanism.

On the other hand, Ginsburg knew that Trump would keep his word and appoint Trump judges to the Supreme Court, thereby eviscerating the influence of living constitutionalist judges such as herself from advancing progressive agendas aimed at transforming the nation into what no freedom loving American would ever recognize. Justice Scalia certainly understood what Ginsburg and her fellow progressives wearing judges' robes were all about:

> Day by day, case by case, it [a Supreme Court dominated by living constitutionalists] is busy designing a [new] Constitution for a country I do not recognize.[390]

In this regard, Trump never vacillated or apologized for his oft stated goal of filling the federal judiciary with originalist judges that would be true to interpreting the actual words contained in the U.S. Constitution thereby protecting the norms and values of the establishment pillars that made America great and will "Keep America Great!" Long after President Trump is gone, this will be his greatest legacy and he will unquestionably cause future objective historians to mark him as one of the greatest presidents this nation has ever seen.

---

[390] Bd. of Cty. Comm'rs v. Umbehr, 518 U.S. 668, 688–89, 711 (1996) (Scalia, J., dissenting).

About the Author

Jeffrey F. Addicott is a Professor of Law and the Director of the Warrior Defense Project at St. Mary's University School of Law, San Antonio, Texas, where he teaches a variety of courses to include National Security Law and Terrorism Law. An active duty Army officer in the Judge Advocate General's Corps for twenty years (he retired in 2000 at the rank of Lieutenant Colonel), Professor Addicott spent a quarter of his career as the senior legal advisor to the United States Army's Special Forces. He is an internationally recognized authority in terrorism law, Professor Addicott not only lectures and participates in professional and academic organizations both in the United States and overseas, he is a frequent contributor to national and international media outlets.

Foreign presentations include numerous professional lectures at universities and government institutions in India, China, Sultanate of Oman, Colombia, Peru, Ukraine, Germany, France, Austria, Canada, Thailand, Japan, Honduras, Haiti, Egypt, Kuwait, Panama, Guatemala, Albania, Okinawa, Cuba, South Korea, England, Mexico, Sweden, Ireland, Scotland, Greece, Israel, Russia, Poland, and Uruguay. Presentations in the United States include over 900 appearances at universities, public and private State and Federal institutions, as well as more than 5,000 appearances on radio, print, and television broadcasts to include the *Wall Street Journal, New York Times, Washington Post, Miami Herald, Dallas Star-Tribune, San Antonio Express-News, Los Angeles Times, Chicago Tribune, Washington Times, Washington Examiner*, FOX News Channel, MSNBC, CNN, ABC, PBS, NBC, CBS, NPR, BBC, OAN, Voice of Russia, and al-Jazeera.

Professor Addicott is a prolific author, publishing over sixty books, articles, and monographs on a variety of legal topics. Among his many contributions to the field, Professor

Addicott pioneered the teaching of law of war and human rights courses to the militaries of numerous nascent democracies in Eastern Europe and Latin America. For these efforts he was awarded the Legion of Merit, named the "Army Judge Advocate of the Year" and honored as a co-recipient of the American Bar Association's Hodson Award.

Dr. Addicott served as the Associate Dean for Administration and Finance at St. Mary's University School of Law (2006-2007) and as the Director of the Center for Terrorism Law (2003-2019). He is also the 2007 recipient of St. Mary's University Alumni Association's "St. Mary's University School of Law Distinguished Faculty Award." Lieutenant Colonel Addicott served in senior legal positions in Germany, Korea, Panama, and throughout the United States. Professor Addicott holds a Doctor of Juridical Science (SJD) and Master of Laws (LLM) from the University of Virginia School of Law. He also received a Master of Laws (LLM) from the Judge Advocate General's School, a Juris Doctor (JD) from the University of Alabama School of Law and a Bachelor of Arts with "Honors in Government" (BA) from the University of Maryland.

Index

A

B

C

D

E

F

G

L

M

N

O

P

Q

R

U

V

W

Y